DANCING
IN THE SHADOW
OF TYRANNY

AN ACTIVIST'S GUIDE TO INNER DISARMAMENT

by
Neriah Lothamer
WWW.NERIAHLOTHAMER.COM

Elite Books
Author's Publishing Cooperative
Santa Rosa, CA 95403
www.Elitebooks.biz

Library of Congress Cataloging-in-Publication Data:

Lothamer, Roger,
      Dancing in the shadow of tyranny : an activists guide to inner
      disarmament / Neriah Lothamer. -- 1st ed.
      p. cm.
      ISBN 0-9720028-8-X

      1. Self-realization--Social aspects. 2. Social change--Psychological aspects.
      3. Lothamer, Neriah. I. Title
BF637.S4L685
158.1--dc22
                              2004026116

Cover and Interior design by Authors Publishing Cooperative
All photographs courtesy of Neriah Lothamer
Typeset in Copperplate and Hoeffler Text
Printed in USA
First Edition

10 9 8 7 6 5 4 3 2 1

CONTENTS

The experience of Eternity right here and now is the function of Life.
— JOSEPH CAMPBELL

DEDICATION

This book is dedicated to my children. You are the real inspiration in my life. Please forgive me if I have not been there enough for you. Know that what I did in life as an activist, visionary, and save-the-world fanatic was motivated by my undying love for you and my burning desire to make this world one you and your children's children could live in and enjoy. Forgive me for what I did that let you down in any way. I realize my mistakes in making any cause more important than being present with you and available to you. Without you all in my life I would have been only a lost and selfish soul; with you in my life I was motivated to make your future worthwhile for generations to come. The love in my heart for you has never dwindled and now is a roaring fire that motivates my every moment. I thank you for loving me. My prayer is that divinity grace you with awareness of its omnipresence. May you know love, both knowing what it feels like to be truly loved and what it feels like to be able to truly love another. Be brave, be fearless, make truth your constant companion, respect all forms of life, and know that you are not separated from god/goddess. In the Rainbow Family we have a saying, "Love everyone, trust a few, and learn to paddle your own canoe." This is the best advice I could give anyone about life.

ACKNOWLEDGMENTS

My deepest thanks and appreciation go to the Great Spirit, the nameless One of a million names, the divine presence in this eternal moment. My beloved companion throughout life, my refuge in sorrow and stress, my solace during the darkest nights of my soul—these are but a few of the ways this love for God has manifest in my life.

In writing this book I have many people to thank for their support and encouragement, most of all my dearest friend on the path of light, Cristina. She has shared her wisdom with me, lighting my way in times of doubt and despair. The well of our relationship is aligned in focus on the spirit of love and truth. What I share here has manifested with her help for which I will be forever grateful. Also, I always will appreciate the love, support, and the sharing of children with Joy, my friend and wife of eighteen years. She was the first to really teach me about love, true love of heartfelt giving. Her comraderie and partnership has been a saving grace in my life. She is a most excellent mother, a great teacher, and a terrificly brave mountain climber; I will always respect and love her. My son Manny is the main person who inspired me to start on this book. He suggested I write a story about the last 10 years, starting with the breakup of our family, and relating what happened to me during that time. I adopted the context of the war on Iraq and the correlation with my father's bullying behavior and the anger inside me that lead to my leaving my family. Thanks to Manny for his love and encouragement. There are so many people I could name here for their support and love, let it suffice for now that these four represent them all and may I be excused from the long listing of names and allowed to say, "Thank you with all my heart." Also, a special appreciation and gratitude to Geralyn Gendreau for her expert editing, technical help, and spiritual slant on the whole project. And especially Dawson Church, thank you for inspiring me to finish writing and publish; your "Cheerio" is awesome.

INTRODUCTION

Now that I have finished writing this book, I return to its beginning with the hope of capturing your interest and inspiring you to read it. It is also here that I pause because I have read and digested all that follows—and in the reading I have found a surprisingly profound and deeply touching voice in the edited versions that tempered the passion of my first drafts. Too much passion can overwhelm, even while too little leaves life insipid.

I know that if I were to read this book for the first time I would be impressed with the eloquent flow of ideas and the practical applications to daily life of the myriad of personal growth situations described. But life itself is not an edited experience. It catches us off-guard, with dangling participles and incomplete sentences. When we take what we know and say it in erudite sophisticated language then we stand a chance of being heard by more folks. Of course, we must also have something useful to share, some significant information that is valuable to someone else's understanding. I don't exactly know how to do that, but the image of a soft-spoken, smiling cowboy, named Will Rogers, springs to my mind. I can see him twirling his rope and doing lariat tricks with it while he talks humorously about current affairs. Sometimes it has felt to me like he is looking over my shoulder as I write, encouraging me to be fearless, to tell it like it is, yet not be so bleak that I lose my sense of humor. The gentle but direct-to-the-point humor with which Will Rogers entertained his audiences is legendary. I don't know any rope tricks, but if Will were here today, I know he would want you to read this book, for the sake of all life on Earth.

This book contains the most important lessons of my life and I feel an overwhelming need to share them. This is because I was raised by a bully (call him "terrorist," "tyrant," or whatever you want, his behavior was characterized by abusive violence), and I became an activist against political and environmental bullies. I believe that, today on Earth, our biggest problem is human bullying. As the Hopi say, "The attitude on

Earth that most needs healing is the one that thinks it knows better than everyone else and forces its way on others."

I define myself often as a visionary activist. When I look up the word "visionary" in the dictionary, it seems to be a degrading term for impractical people who have delusions and see things that are not there. Personally, I always had a more romanticised understanding that probably came from reading the Bible and hanging out with Bohemians: I believe that a visionary is someone who has had a bona fide spiritual insight, a vision, and bases the rest of his or her life around that insight. Thus a visionary to me is someone who lives the vision seen in their highest and most lucid states. The dictionary definition is probably the more accepted version. Whether history bears out the significance of LSD, Timothy Leary, Baby Boomers, the Grateful Dead, and the naive media of the 1960's as true evolutionary landmarks, or whether the whole Flower Child era was merely a fad, millions of us experienced it first-hand and will always know that there is another way of looking at events.

This book is a collection of thoughts and reflections about waking up out of the nightmare perpetuated by tyranny. It is about human evolution and personal revelation. Gandhi said, "We must become the change we seek." Today, I say, "We are the change we seek."

My personal journey has involved deep explorations into how we experience ourselves, why the energy to dominate or be dominated is so prevalent in our lives, and why anger and fear perpetuate themselves. Eva Pierrakos introduced the term forcing current to highlight the human tendency to use forcefulness to get our way. Gary Zukav drew a distinction as to the difference between external power and authentic power. Where does authentic power come from? And what does this have to do with the fear that keeps our political system so ravaged by corruption? The quality of life on our planet depends greatly on how we reconcile these questions.

This book is a personal study of myself and the world around me. I notice and point out the similarities between our individual lives and the world's politics. I ask questions that seek a path of peace and common sense. I reflect on what is not working anymore, trends that humanity recognizes need changing—global warming resulting from our polluting fuels, finding non-violent solutions to war, balancing our economic and political systems between haves and have-nots, and our attitudes toward freedom, democracy, voting, and terrorism.

Fear, terror, anger, abuse, power—these are the real issues in our world and in our relationships. The issues and the influences that are evolving and involving humanity now are very challenging. In this book I look at the complexity of life on Earth today and how to come up with simple, easy-to-understand solutions to our collective and personal problems. Bullying energy in particular is addressed as I especially see a connection in my life between the tyranny of child abuse and the bigger picture of twenty-first century humanity.

This is a difficult subject to address. I seek optimistic and non-authoritarian solutions, ones that all humans might agree with. I seek peace on Earth and an end to suffering and abuse. I look for people of like mind to work with and I encourage all of us to dedicate ourselves to the healing of our world. I draw upon my activism and explorations of alternative lifestyles, but I also share the resources that helped me to mature: R. Buckminister Fuller, Marshal B. Rosenberg, Eva Pierrakos, Ramana Maharshi, Papaji, Gandhi, Teilhard de Chardin, Yogananda, Milton H. Erickson, Stephen W. Hawking, and others. I draw from the well of our collective knowledge to find fresh water instead of rotting slime. The future looks to me as though humanity is about to massively connect with its true authentic power rather than the "forcing current" we are used to. The reasons are more and more obvious as we read the newspapers about all the pollution, environmental destruction, war, and violence in our world

Solutions are necessary, options must be considered, and strategies need to be implemented. This book looks at these needs and considers what resources we have to meet them, especially the resources inside of us that we can each apply in our personal lives as well as to our collective life on Earth. I have only my experience to share with you here. I have no other agenda. I don't work for the military-industrial complex, politicians, or special interest groups. I have six grown children. I would like to hope that their children have a future on this planet that is peaceful and healthy. I pray that this book helps that to be. In fact, that is exactly what this book is about; it is my attempt to save the world. I believe that if you read this you will be moved and inspired to participate in the greatest act of love that has ever manifested on our planet—the prophesied "Heaven on Earth."

LOVE IS ALWAYS A CHOICE

by Neriah Lothamer

The transformation of the world,
     and the Earth
          and our own consciousness,
             our focus and will;
these are all the same thing:
our attitude towards ourselves as beings of Light in a universe of Love.
How many directions and dimensions we can perceive ourselves
astonishes us as it unfolds.
Love is always a choice
...a choice of perception.
To explore all dimensions of love is to live forever.
Thank you, Great Spirit and Earth Mother, for this sacred breath.
     Every one sacred
          a meeting and a door between two worlds,
             a giving and taking,
               a way of awakening.
Love is always a choice
     ...a choice of perception.

1

THE NEW CHIVALRY

You, who are on the road must have a code that you can live by.
—CROSBY, STILLS, NASH, AND YOUNG

*A*s I climb to the crest of the hill, the deep blue sky opens out over a lush green valley. Birds fly around my head and swoop down to drink from the gently flowing river in the valley's floor. The air is clean, filled with the shifting fragrances of wild flowers. I find the shade of a large tree inviting. I sit on the soft, lush grass, and lean against the tree trunk, looking out over the beautiful valley.

People in colorful costumes dance and sing, parading through a grassy meadow near the river. Sprinkled along the path are numerous tipis, yurts, geodesic domes, Bedouin tents, and brightly colored canopies. I see people of all races: Tibetans, Hindus, Native Americans, Africans, Europeans, Asians, and indigenous people, a truly international celebration. This beautiful, colorful display of humanity's diverse spiritual cultures parading together strikes a thrilling cord in the depths of my being.

Musicians and drummers blend diverse textures and heavenly harmonies. Like angelic conductors, they inspire other voices to naturally join in and sing along. Dancers parade with colorful banners, flags, costumes, and streaming ribbons. Brightly colored kites and balloons fill the air with festive anticipation. Baton twirlers, clowns, stilt-walkers, and giant puppets gesture for all to join in the

15

joyful throng. With painted faces and fancy costumes, a procession of dancing children cheers with delight as they enter the parade. Smiling, happy people are everywhere.

As she enters a huge, circular meadow, the old Native American woman leading the parade blows a conch. The low, deep sound trumpets long and loud down the valley. A chorus of echoing conch shells replies from the surrounding hills. Holding a bundle of smoking sage, the old woman circles the meadow four times chanting a prayer. Then she walks to the center of the circle and raises a long-stemmed pipe covered with medicine feathers high above her head, pointing to the sky. A group of people carries a large wooden pole to the spot where she stands in the center of the meadow. Beautifully bedecked with ribbons and feathers, the pole has been carved with religious symbols and words of peace from many different cultures. More people come, carrying rocks to stack around the base of the pole and secure it upright.

The parade enters, and celebrants circle around the edges of the meadow until the space is filled with thousands. The drumming reaches a crescendo. The crowd roars. Then, all become silent and everyone sits down. The elder woman remains standing, looking at the top of the pole, holding her pipe aloft. Silently, she moves the pipe in prayer to the seven sacred directions. When she finishes her invocation, she places the pipe at the foot of the pole and sits down next to it in silence.

A peaceful quiet pervades the meadow. People are rapt in prayer. Minutes become hours as the silence deepens; a profound state of collective reverence is reached. When the sun is at high noon, a low humming sound begins. The hum grows and grows and for twenty minutes, thousands of voices join in a powerful, harmonious hum that finally bursts into a climax of hoops, hollers, and alleluias. Musicians and drummers resume their lively jubilee. People stroll, talk, and dance, serenaded by the spontaneous orchestra. As the afternoon grows late, an early dinner is brought out, another prayer is shared, and all sit down in concentric circles to communion at the meal.

As I look over the surrounding hills, I see the graceful movement of a beautiful woman dancing through the forest. Her dance is fluid, effortless, and utterly natural as she drifts through the trees. Entranced by her grace, I watch for a while, enjoying the delight her dance inspires in my heart and mind. Several minutes pass before I realize this angel is not simply dancing her joy: she is picking up litter! I am so inspired that I joyfully pick up trash wherever I go throughout the rest of my day.

Everyone I meet bears a welcoming smile. Folks hauling food and supplies on their backs smile with beaming awareness. Latrine diggers, woodchoppers, and kitchen crews work happily in service of community needs. Circles of people cluster around, sharing healing techniques, stories, visions, and speaking their highest hopes and dreams. Volunteers are first entertained and then enlisted by a colorful cast of characters. Community health and safety needs are portrayed in a theatrical, artful display. A tangible spirit of co-operation makes taking care of basic community needs natural and easy with plenty of time left over for teaching, learning, playing, enjoying, appreciating, trading, creating, storytelling, entertaining, healing, and praying together.

Is this a utopian dream? Is it a peace-lover's futuristic fantasy?

The events herein described are neither fiction, nor fantasy. They are an aggregate of actual experiences I have had over the past thirty-two years. The events did not spring out of imagination, but out of personal experience. When common sense in the midst of these experiences demanded that I function in a responsible way, I could and did. I cooked, changed diapers, dug latrines, chopped wood, and put out forest fires—often without electricity or automobiles, and in the company of thousands of others. I am not describing an alternate universe; although such gatherings are certainly an alternate reality to the common everyday world we call "life" in these United States.

I have attended many such events. Along with the exhilaration of gathering together, the awe of sharing community alternatives, and the inspiration of evolving a whole new human social system, comes a tremendous amount of work. The work involves much more than manual labor; it involves the hard work of communication.

CHAPTER ONE

How do twenty thousand people—with children—survive as a cohesive community in the wilds? Group co-ordination is required, as are many agreements about how to keep our food and water safe for consumption, and our women and children clear of danger. Learning how to keep the peace is essential. And all it takes, oddly enough, are two things humans possess in ample supply: common sense and imagination.

Common sense says that people are just people, that we all have basic needs. Take care of basic human needs and the rest is up to individual free will. Common sense also tells us that one person's freedom ends where it deprives another of his or her freedom. But we need imagination to apply common sense at large gatherings. And we need common sense to temper imagination. We need the ability to perceive reality without the blinding veil of mental concepts that also makes good use of the gut feelings that come through our solar plexus. Common sense is the radar that helps us navigate without getting sunk by hidden dangers under the surface. In many ways, the gatherings described above can be seen as a collaborative experiment in right imagination or right mindfulness as taught by the Buddha. These events have shown me what is possible for humanity. By combining common sense and imagination we *can* live in harmony. We can evolve systems that care for our basic human needs by applying our collective imagination tempered with common sense. To do this, we share a code of ethics that comes from our prayers to bring the peace of Heaven on Earth, and that code of ethics comes from the Code of Life.

The Code of Life is in our DNA, in our blood, in our cells. Expressed in the highest values humans share in common, the Code of Life defines the ways of the physical universe: the parameters and principles by which matter and energy manifest. These principles have evolved human consciousness; they completely compose, support, and sustain human consciousness. They are fundamental truths of the universe that existed before humans, and will continue when humans are gone.

The human heart pulses through an alliance of forces that rule stars as well as atoms—forces that create complex human organisms and develop within them a capacity for consciousness. Whether conceived as deities or "the one true God" by human definition, these forces are everywhere, in everything. The principles they enforce permeate our experience: physical, mental, emotional, and spiritual. Evolution meets humanity head-on with these principles, challenging us to recycle our traditional values and beliefs.

Although humanity's moral and ethical codes have their roots in history, the current values of humanity are in a vast transition. Our twenty-first century world is an ever-accelerating whirlwind of change. Mayan prophecies suggest an exponential acceleration in human evolution at this time. Humans are discovering more in all dimensions because of this accelerated growth of knowledge and technology, a phenomenon we must understand as both internal and external.

Julian Huxley said, "In mankind, evolution is conscious of itself." What if the goal of evolution is the consciousness possible in the human cerebral cortex? What if our consciousness-of-self is what gives evolution the resource to achieve spiritual awareness? Teilhard de Chardin, a Roman Catholic priest active in the early and mid-twentieth century, was a world-renowned expert in the fields of botany, biology, anthropology, and archaeology. He believed the conscious unification of spirit and matter to be the purpose of evolution. He suggested humans are not only capable of this consciousness individually, but also collectively. "It is the Spirit of Evolution which, suppressing the spirit of egoism, is of its own right springing to new life in our hearts, and in such a way as to counteract those elements in the forces of collectivization which are poisonous to life."[1] De Chardin suggested that the human capacity to gather information and to reflect upon it, individually and collectively, creates a collective consciousness that will eventually lead individuals to see themselves as a cell in the collective body of humanity.

Silenced by his order of Jesuits for his radical views, and forbidden to publish his work, de Chardin wrote letters, which were passed around underground and eventually published. The "mystical body of Christ" and the "second coming" or "paroushia" as de Chardin called it, are all the same thing. He believed the second coming meant individual enlightenment and awareness of the Christ within, coupled with an awareness of the same Christ in others, in humanity as a whole,[3] and in all life on Earth.

CHAPTER ONE

Teilhard de Chardin's mystical understanding of evolution shows Western mystics how to embrace evolutionary theory as something spiritual rather than materialistic. The transformation of the world is the same as the transformation of each person, and changes are crucial and profound in both. We are evolution conscious of itself, evolution seeking fusion of spirit and matter. This understanding ennobles our spirit, and transforms the context in which we live.

It is July 4, 2004. Twenty thousand people sit silently in a forest meadow for the annual prayer gathering. The silence is awesome. Birds sing in the trees. The breeze of early morning rises through the grass. A profound stillness begins to envelop my heart, but I am struggling with anger. Two old friends sit near me in the circle, the very two my anger has grudged throughout the last year. I judge them for betraying the trust of friendship and being malicious. I feel like hitting, hurting, berating, screaming, and yes, even that old feeling inside of wanting to kill haunts me as I try to pray. I am suddenly aware that my struggle is exactly what humanity, as a whole, needs to heal to bring peace to the world.

I know I am responsible for my experience, and that blame does not serve anyone. I begin to accept reality. I feel an opening in my heart; the light of peace relaxes me. I am aware that in oneness is diversity and within divinity is all possibility. I remember my commitment to revere the divine in everyone. I let go of judgments, realizing that discernment is more appropriate. This helps me to accept and love my friends despite my dislike of their behavioral choices, which have shown me I need to stay safely out of range.

I begin to imagine integrity as a code of ethics. Evolutionary forces seem to coalesce with my prayers in this meadow. I feel human, archetypal, and spiritual currents moving between the people in the circle and all across this planet. My turbulent emotions calm down and I feel peace again.

Evolution meets something new in the human cerebral cortex: imagination. Every law, rule, religion, belief, and value originates in the imagination of the human mind. Through human imagination and human belief, evolution deals its hand. People who lived a hundred years ago would have been stunned into disbelief if a time travel machine allowed them to drop in on your typical day. How shocked might we be if the same time machine could afford us a glimpse of what will be a hundred years hence? Imagining this, I see two clear scenarios, both of which demand a better code of conduct for humanity.

The first scenario is apocalyptic, wherein the world is almost destroyed and human life takes a giant evolutionary step backwards. The second scenario is the utopian vision: humanity working in natural harmony with each other and the Earth. Innumerable scenarios exist between these extremes, but all point out the need for a better code, one that diverts our current path of global suicide.

This is not the first time in human history the demand for a code of honor has been felt. A similar demand brought forward a code of decency and respect known as Chivalry at a time when armored men on tall warhorses could hack up anyone standing in their way. To kill and ride out of town with whatever they could claim was all too easy. Men would plunder, pillage, rape, burn, murder, scorn, torture, and enslave in the belief that "might is right." Chivalry emerged to extol the merits of using force judiciously and only to defend oneself and the helpless. As a set of principles to which a man could aspire, it refined men's behavior and defined Knighthood, a societal position of honor.

The emerging code of humanity likewise requires we summon chivalrous refinements of character, such as gallantry, courtesy, and respectful attention to women and children. The new code is different in many ways to Chivalry, however, and must be designed for our time. Blind obedience to any church is no more appropriate than blind obedience to a liege lord. *Devotion to divinity within each person is preferable to blind obedience to organized religion.* This is a radical change we would do well to recognize, for it is a radical change in our understanding of the Code of Life. Compelled by the evolutionary forces of fusion, humanity must reject the divisionary and separatist aspects of religion. Respect and tolerance for all religions is now required. This revolution in our thinking, attitudes, and beliefs is the result of humanity reflecting on the historical abuses by and of religions. Propelled by the urge toward unification that is motivating us to live more harmoniously, humanity must now use imagination to find religious tolerance, rather than continuing the "holy wars."

Involution evolves and evolution involves. As we process our inner experience, we become more involved in the collective human experience. Involvement happens through awareness that is gained by reflection on our collective experience. Imagination allows us to consider our options. Without imagination, we have no choice but to keep repeating the same mistakes. Imagination is evolution's way of using the human cerebral cortex to achieve the prime directive of conscious unity. Imagination empowers consciousness to reflect upon what has yet to be experienced and made manifest.

Evolution meets imagination with common sense. Without common sense as a reality check, imagination would run off on any number of tangents. Common sense not only means common to all but accessible to all. This is why the new code is based on the Code of Life. The Code of Life can be found everywhere and all creation recognizes its principles.

The New Chivalry reveals how to communicate; how to speak and listen with respect and attention; it shows us the heart of consensus. Communication can solve any problem. Consensus, and the circumspect point of view it brings, allows communities to get needed support to solve their problems. This takes time to learn, but the "how to" of communicating clearly and learning to listen with compassionate consideration is essential to this emerging code.

The New Chivalry reveals the way of peaceful non-violence. It shows how to achieve peace and non-violence in words and deeds. It shows how to start with ourselves and create a peaceful life experience. It identifies the problem areas within us that bring distress and turmoil, the exact problem areas that erupt violently in our language and behavior toward others. It does all this by revealing the natural love in our hearts, the affection that inspires our respect and consideration for others.

Through love, the code reveals how we can experience our world and ourselves in a healthy, happy, and harmonious manner. When we love someone enough to learn not to hit them angrily, not to threaten them, not to sexually abuse them, and not to yell at them; then we *feel* like changing. Unless we really feel the love within us, we will not change our harmful behaviors for long.

To love God by praying before statues is easy compared to loving God in people. *The devotion required to see God in each person and in all things is challenging, and stretches the soul to embrace what is hardest to accept.* When we revere the essential "Buddha nature" in even the most unenlightened; we can accept that our own evil exists within the omnipresence of God. To deny evil is to empower it. When we face evil in ourselves and in others, we loosen its strong hold. Facing evil can only be done by simultaneously facing divinity. It is the divinity within us, struggling with the bestial values and beliefs of our ancestors, that can imagine new ways to ensure survival now.

We, as the human part of evolution, must learn to control our childish tyrannical behavior before we destroy ourselves. In her Pathwork lectures, Eva Pierrakos said, "Humanity has now left behind infancy and childhood. It is just about coming through its adolescence, but is not yet a mature, adult entity."[2] Humanity is changing its values, seeking more mature freedoms, and learning about self-responsibility and partnership. As a race, we are at war with ourselves, divided by contradictory views, confused by philosophical and cultural splits. As Pierrakos points out, "The organism which, in perfection, could and will function harmoniously, in union with itself, must be at war with itself as long as it is divided within by unrealistic concepts, wrong conclusions, self-centered and infantile pursuits, limited outlooks, lack of concern, subjectivity and unfairness due to blind, isolating tendencies; the individual human body, soul, and spirit is identical with the body, soul and spirit of humanity as a whole."

According to Pierrakos, the abuses of humanity's collective past need to be healed, as well as each one's personal past. Humanity must consciously examine the ugliest memories it has sealed behind denial.

To enter into this global self-examination means accepting that history has been rewritten by each conquering culture to show their version of the facts. To do this we must be willing to see our favorite superstitions revealed as just that: superstition, not fact.

CHAPTER ONE

Awareness is now demanded by mama evolution, awareness that both takes responsibility for the past and looks to the future. When we wake up in an auto going downhill out of control with no-one in the driver's seat, pointing the finger of blame or trying to escape will not work. Times like this demand fast action and force us to mature, first by *recognizing* that we have the ability to respond and second, by *choosing* to respond with swift, decisive action.

The only way I know to feel responsibility is to tune into love: love for myself, divinity, humanity, those dear to me, and life on Earth. Love is not lust or selfish pleasure. It is an experience that reaches into my soul, stretches deep into my body, and erupts in my heart with tears of bliss. Love makes me feel like saving the world.

The challenge to all humanity is to love now more than ever. This love is not the "gimme" type of love, but a *giving* that spontaneously springs from the heart. This love needs no forcing, coaxing, cajoling, or manipulation. This love knows no fear. This love accepts the challenge of bringing true and lasting peace among the nations. This love rolls up its shirtsleeves and exuberantly exclaims, "We can do it!"

Humanity is not "you" or "I"—humanity is "we." Humanity is not divisive, but inclusive. We all share in this adventure; within each of us is the source that manifests this moment in time and space. Humanity is a parade of diversity we all walk in, as well as a parade of resources we all check out in time. Human nature is humanity's nature; it is "our" nature. This human nature is parading now toward changing values. This human nature is you and I and everyone else lifting their eyes toward those banners that lead the parade, and saying, in our hearts, with them:

"We are the sources of all movements, the mothers of all gatherings, and the creators of all religions. We have spawned the visionary Bohemian rhapsody of love, freedom, and beauty throughout the world. We bring joy everywhere with our entertaining way of enlightening everything on our path."

"We have opened the hearts of children who seek the truth about life and Earth and spirit. We have shown them how to follow spirit where it leads and to give thanks for what we can share together. We

have brought the elders of the ancient ones to speak to our children and we carry their teachings everywhere we go. The Mayan calendar, the Hopi prophecies, the legends of indigenous Americans, religious revelations; all these tell of and prove our existence. We are here now to point to the light in each and every human, we invoke its activation; we beseech and coax and cajole and urge it to come forward in all its brightness, and shine."

"We are the drummers, the artists, the musicians, the feeders of the poor and homeless, the gypsies, the eccentric and colorfully dressed, the monks and priestesses, the goddesses and the highest of the holy laborers. We can leap in divine bliss as we dance through our lives. We are the result of humanity's deepest prayers, we are the children of light and peace and love."

"Love, and the oneness it pulses with, is our heart beating with the eternal prime directive of evolution. We are pointing to this light of love, and inviting humanity to join in the greatest miracle of love that has ever happened: peace on Earth."

Now we begin to express the love of which humanity is really capable, love incarnate.

2
AWAKENING FROM TYRANNY

And the vision that was planted in my brain
Still remains
Within the sounds of silence.
—SIMON AND GARFUNKEL

Sex, money, power—all within my grasp. I feel them as active forces, enticing my will to reach for more, more, more. A current of desire consumes me in a fury of lust. This current has run through my entire life, holding my body, mind, and heart captive. But in my soul, I feel a deeper call, a hunger so compelling that I fall into it and am devoured. My body is no longer mine. My mind belongs to all humanity. My heart is an ocean and I swim in its waves of emotion. I stand, naked, stripped of all disguise, facing rape and death. I am bound and fettered by authority's greed. I face my oppressor. In the mirror that surrounds me I see only myself—no saint or sinner, just another human being. I see a man with human fears and hopes. I reach out to touch the lips of my reflection. I want to hear. I seek to know. I pray that words will come from the source of all truth, all honesty. May my life be spared and may my loved ones be happy. Suddenly the mirror shatters into several billion fragments, each reflecting something different yet the same. My heart screams in compassion. My mind wails at the irrationality of the world. My eyes franticly look for hope and my curiosity explodes. I must know if others care!

CHAPTER TWO

If I could look the whole world in the eye and ask one question, I would say, "What is life on Earth worth to you?"

It is February 2003 and I am stuck near Los Angeles; a business deal has just gone sour. My associates can't seem to communicate. My insides feel like they are being gnawed on by a small rat. I am suddenly out of the loop, my business partners will not tell me what is going on, and my impatience is mounting into rage. I look around frantically for someplace to unwind—the traffic shows no mercy. Signs, locked gates, guards, and fences zoom by. L.A.'s generic neighborhoods offer no sanctuary. Finally, I see a sign for a state park, a beach, and pull into the parking lot. It is early and the beach is deserted. I lock my car, look around, and smell the clean ocean breeze. The traffic is a small droning blur in the background and the path to the beach buffers the chaos of the city. I follow the winding trail to the viewpoint at the top of the cliffs and then head down the wood and sand stairs to the beach. I walk aimlessly. I do not really think—thoughts bombard me. I feel shell-shocked. My best friend has just turned against me on a very important deal we've been working on for months. Betrayal, treachery, denial, lies, dishonest games—my thoughts won't stop. My girlfriend is talking about leaving me, I've just been ripped off, and it seems my only option is to find a cheap hotel and twiddle my thumbs. I'm so angry I could scream.

The sea is a welcome sight. Rows of mighty waves cascade to the beach. The gulls circle the rocks and skim the sand on their endless orbits out to sea and back. I watch while they catch the wind and hover a moment before gliding on. I breathe deeply, wrestling with my raging feelings and trying to find some calm. But my thoughts still haunt me. I wasted all that time and energy; can I recover from this financial blow? Even my love life sucks. Sitting down on the rocky promontory, I see the glistening light on the foamy tops of the waves as they continue past me to beat upon the shore. I wonder how I can be so blind and why people are so cruel.

§ § §

I spend the next several days in total agony, without a moment of peace. Like a prisoner waiting for the recess bell, I am bored and eager to do anything else. I endure excruciating emotions that tear me inside out. I cry, moan, bitch, wail, and despair until there is nothing left.

A group of kids in the motel room next door are getting more and more drunk. I hear them egging each other on, daring each other to go out on Hollywood Boulevard and score with a prostitute. I can hear the macho voices through the thin walls, taunting each other, "Come on, homeboy, we came this far, you chicken shit to fuck a bitch?" Eventually they leave and I sit alone in the dark quiet, breathing deeply as I try to still the raging beast inside me. The beasts on the street outside are raging too—strange faces, homeless people, and dirty, poor, undernourished, over-intoxicated, conniving, and scheming hordes of humanity. Are we all just unoriginal reproductions of true humans?

My thirty-dollar room is my only buffer, my only refuge, and my last sanctuary. I look desperately for an answer: what are these feelings erupting inside me? I'm going to lose control. I feel like a complete and total lunatic! What is going on? What is the answer? How can I possibly survive another moment of this hell?

§ § §

A week later, I'm back at home. The homecoming left much to be desired. Everyone around me disgusts me. My friend has revealed that his lack of integrity is deliberate. My girlfriend wants to go live with a masseur she finds attractive—I suspect they may already be having an affair. Yo-yoing between complete depression and suicidal mass murder, I sit down, breathe deeply, and try to quiet the storm. A friend comes in from a trip to town, talking excitedly, "The President just announced they are going to start bombing Iraq!" As she reads the headlines, I feel a wave of disgust. My anger snowballs again into a rage and starts to roll down a hill. The snowball turns into an avalanche as my rage takes on planetary proportions.

§ § §

A few days later, I sense a distinct revolutionary moment as 300,000 people make their presence felt in San Francisco's streets. We parade through downtown carrying thousands of signs protesting the forthcoming invasion of Iraq. We are not alone. Worldwide, in dozens of other nations, people are gathered in solidarity to protest the impending bombing. Joan Baez is among the crowd today, as are many of my original radical comrades—so many signs, so many years since Vietnam. Will we ever convince them to slow the war machine down? Shades of the sixties, it brings tears to my eyes as I think of brothers lost in 'Nam, innocent children murdered, and families torn apart by oppression and war.

Suddenly the thought occurs to me that at this very moment there are more people gathered worldwide for peace than ever before. Never in history have this many people publicly displayed their protest against war. A chill rushes up my spine and I feel connected to the power of the event. What is happening? Why am I feeling such strong emotions? Why am I feeling so rebellious against the parent culture, against big brother and his bullyboys? Bullyboys—that is what we called them at rock and roll shows. They are meaner than any troublemaker. They are the security guards, the cops, and the army. The ones who move "the trouble" to a quarantined place, so folks can get on with business as usual.

§ § §

Now, two days later, it is happening. Million dollar missiles are exploding in some Iraqi kid's yard. "Official" information saturates the network television stations and corporately owned radio waves. Meanwhile, on the Internet, millions upload and download a more accurate picture of the war. The streets are full. San Francisco is at a standstill; the downtown area is a gridlock. Battalions of police follow the waves of protesters. Thousands of demonstrators stand face-to-face with the cops and I hear talk about trashing the federal building. Finally, the protesters surround the police. After a pregnant, uneasy pause, the cops relax. There will be no violence. This is a peace march. The protesters line up, and one by one, demand to be arrested. I wonder why? What is going on?

§ § §

It is August 2003, my fifty-seventh birthday. I have just learned that my father died last March, when the Iraq bombing was hitting the headlines. He died of old age; at least that's my guess. We hadn't communicated but half a dozen times in twenty years. I feel shocked that I could be so out of touch. I didn't even know he was ill. More shocking still: no one in my family was able to track me down. I feel very strange knowing that my father has been dead for several months and I had no idea.

My father's death brings into focus the link between my anger about the war and the rage I feel toward bullies. My dad was a bully. It strikes me as a strange coincidence that he died just as another war atrocity began. Somehow, I feel that the energy of tyranny has loosened its grip on me. I feel free of the yoke of repression and I intend to stay that way.

My anger has begun to change shape, like a spent volcano, no longer fuming — an empty shell of cooled liquid stone. The anger management, and non-violent communication trainings, have clearly helped. Little cracks of light are appearing through my dark clouds; wisps of understanding greet me almost daily. I feel renewed and restored, saner than I can remember. The heart of anger has opened its inner chamber of secrets to me; the secret power of tyranny, the power to bully and murder, has revealed its hidden truths to me.

Tyranny is a leftover rotting in the refrigerator.

Our sophisticated and civilized tyranny is also like a baton passed from one rat in the race to another. It is a twisted tradition that once meant something, but the meaning is lost. All the messenger hands off now is a message of unbridled anger.

Tyranny and anger need to be perpetuated, or they wither into impotence. Without some advocate for their cause, some kind of justification given by an authority, they are not able to continue. Like uncouth bullies, they would simply be locked up as a public nuisance.

Perhaps we are not all that different from the humble, easy-going Hobbit who finally realizes that he must take the ring of fear back to its origins and make sure it is destroyed. When we are ready to accept responsibility for our experience and awaken from tyranny, we cannot avoid reality any longer. Mighty battles wage between armies of greater and greater destructive powers, while non-combatants on the spiritual-psychological front inwardly do the real and very hard work of finding within themselves the source of such conflicts.

While we reach deep into the darkness to find the roots of our fears and gain freedom from them, evolution moves us forward in spite of ourselves. Infinity, eternity, spirit, consciousness, awareness, oneness; these are all part of what we experience. The zero field, quantum physics, and string theories have increased our understanding of our world and ourselves. A hundred years ago, people did not have television, cell phones, computers, the Internet, digital media, or credit cards. Most people worked twelve hours a day, seven days a week—and barely survived; they didn't have time, or the information, to think about much else. If we are so much more advanced than we were a hundred years ago, why do we find ourselves cornered by environmental, ecological, and economic emergencies that constantly threaten us? Why are we still playing war games and building more sophisticated weapons when we already possess sufficient destructive power to annihilate every inhabitable corner of the world several times over? What purpose is served by avoiding, and denying, the reality of the impact our species has had on the Earth's biosphere and on our own psycho-sphere? What will it take for us to reflect on this deeply enough to take responsibility and correct our behavior?

Today, every human being lives in a polluted environment. Our decades-old fear of impending nuclear destruction has given way to the fear of terrorists' attacks. Both realities have become a part of the modern psyche. But fear spells profit for many. Clearly, our fear supports the half-trillion-dollar-a-year defense industry. It supports gun manufacturers, arms dealers, and even video war games that children play. It also feeds less obvious "protectors" like doctors, lawyers, counselors, bankers, and insurance agents. More and more people everyday are beginning to realize the fragile future of humanity.

Baby Boomers have come of age. More people with a global sensitivity are alive now than at any other time in history. Most of us are better educated than medieval royalty could have dreamed of, and we live with an affluence afforded formerly only to kings and emperors. When Boomers went to college and discovered LSD, more than a few lights in consciousness came on. And then there was Vietnam. Today, aging Boomers stand with teeth on edge as the war machine threatens to dominate the world. How does such an individual respond to this?

I was born in America in 1946, raised amidst a post World War environment that was historically unprecedented. Millions like me were born into this affluent, victorious war culture. We were the first generation raised on television. By the time we were five years old, instead of nursery rhymes, our heads were full of hip television jingles, touting the newest and best consumer items. Our parents bought the American dream as it was sold to them: fancy new multi-colored cars, nylons and latex girdles, Hi-fidelity sound systems, tiny transistor radios, electric irons with steam, automatic washers and dryers, vacuum cleaners with dozens of attachments, dishwashing machines, and trips to Disneyland.

As our generation approached the end of high school, and threatened to flood the workforce, a national fear arose that unemployment rates would soar out of control. Government-insured student loans, which never existed before, were created, making it easier to go to college. Also, G.I. benefits were reinstated and vets could not only start a business, or buy a home, but they could go to college, too. We were the most educated young minds in all of human history.

In August of 1968, when Boomers invaded Chicago during the Democratic Convention in the hope of getting politicians to listen, we were desperate to be heard in the political process. Banned from the convention itself, we gathered in the streets outside it, talking to the media who were covering the event. Like me, millions watched the protests live on television. As it escalated and the cops moved in to control the mob, we witnessed police brutality begin. We watched billy-clubs smash heads. We watched blood flow in the streets. We watched students who could have been us, who were us, get treated as though they were enemies of the state. We felt outrage erupting inside us. Shock overwhelmed us. Our collective public reaction was a rage of sympathy for the victims. We were changing in that moment from college kids with optimistic hopes into radicals. We were seeing violence, unedited and live, in the streets of Chicago. Every major news source had reporters and cameras there to document the violence. We watched the Chicago police mercilessly beat the protestors—and the war was now in our American streets and in our face.

The next couple of years included a huge series of nationwide campus protests and demonstrations against the war. Students gathered in large numbers and began to mobilize against it in every conceivable way. Some demonstrations were so radical that the National Guard was called to the campus to back up the police. Tension mounted high and on May 4th 1970, in Ohio, at the Kent State University campus, four students were shot and killed by guardsmen, and several others critically wounded.

Our generation reacted to Kent State with unprecedented passion, shutting down every major campus across the country. The lawns of America's universities turned into outdoor meeting halls and conference rooms as we sat on the grass and discussed what to do. For millions of us, those moments of coming together were a sharing of conscience, a time when our country's sense of decency was collectively sensed, our scruples publicly spoken, and we emerged organically and everywhere at once with our peace signs.

Having been raised in a very different atmosphere, with post-Depression worries about getting enough potatoes to feed the children rather than about nuclear bombs, the parents of Baby Boomers scratched their heads in the face of the questions raised by their offspring. When their privileged, well-fed kids burned down ROTC buildings, parental bewilderment turned into hand wringing, berating, and scorn. Our parents simply had no clue as to why we were up in arms—with banners and tie-dies—sticking flowers in soldiers' gun barrels—to put a stop to the Vietnam War. Members of "the older generation" were so comfortably numb, in their hard-won, all-American affluence, that they could not relate to the havoc-filled devastation and poverty the war was wreaking on a faraway world. Their values clashed mightily with those of their children. On billboards across the country, the National Student Union posted signs stating, "Mom and Dad, your silence is killing us."

The crass materialism of post-WW II America set the stage for the emergence of the flower children. Challenging our elders, we set out to establish spiritual values beyond religion. Love, peace, and spiritual oneness became hallmarks of Boomers. As the value shifted away from materialism, new businesses emerged to cater to that new market. And as the spiral turned, anti-materialists found their own roads into the materialistic way.

But the life well lived cannot be all about philosophy and politics. At some point, we all are compelled to look inside ourselves or die in the denial and ignorance of blame. When this transition occurred for me, my personal struggle to save the world from war turned into a heartbreaking vigil to protect the human tribe from the most evil tyrant imaginable: me. Little did I know, as a fire-breathing young activist, that the bully inside of me was what I was going up against. Like many young minds, I blamed my parents and the politics of their generation for the mess. I blamed the Church and its centuries of oppression, and I wagged a righteous finger at the Inquisition. I railed at a government that blatantly killed despite having their war-mongering exposed on the news night after night. I screamed at the nuclear arsenals. I marched with hundreds of thousands in the streets. But never did I pause to feel the tyrant inside. I was blind to how it ran me.

The first sign of change came when I had kids. We raised them, for a time in a school bus, while we did the circuit hippie-style—visiting new age communities, traveling to gatherings, festivals, rallies, and rock concerts—in the hopes of finding a viable alternative to the parent culture. We met native American Indians: wise old women, chiefs, and medicine men. We walked with peace pilgrims praying with each step. We heard the eagles in the mountains as we saw them soar. We sang at the campfires of the free people who gypsy around the country. Eventually, we settled down and our kids grew up. Many of us cut our hair and went to work. Many also continued to be activists. All of us had to take up a personal growth path and begin to digest our lessons in this life. And now, many of us have more than one grandchild on our knee.

Chapter Two

What did the Boomer generation in America learn? What can we offer to the next generation and beyond? What are the feelings of antiwar activists of the Boomer generation today? What thoughts and emotions go through the minds and hearts of forty-year veteran antiwar activists when another Iraq oil war threatens to draft our children? What can humanity now say we know for sure about tyranny and war? What have we learned about peace?

Like every generation, we've learned a great deal about the everyday, human side of life. We've figured out some basics as to how humans might best get along and live with each other. We've asked questions as to how we communicate, and taken note about how well we function when communication hits those inevitable bumps along the road. The communication of our discoveries is an important part of humanity's evolution. If we cannot communicate these answers to ourselves, to our loved ones and friends, or to the world, then we haven't understood the lessons themselves yet.

As for God, and sex, and love, and relationship, over the past quarter-century our generation has spawned a multi-tiered self-help and inspirational industry in the form of books, seminars and on-line advice. Our bookshelves attest to the detailed attention we have paid to learning about these areas of human life. Like every generation, we want to offer our unique insight into the dilemmas faced by human societies' groupings— from nation states to families. We want to put our finger on the pulse of the future and do our best to help all humans, at long last, figure out how to live in peace, how to actually stop killing.

These are big issues begging for big solutions. I don't know more than anyone else. All I can do is remind you of what you already know and, hopefully, inspire you to express it creatively in your corner of the universe. Evolution, the ultimate reality check, seeks only for what is the functional and least boring way to continually evolve. Here we are, evolution aware of itself; the mental aspect of evolution now asking ourselves, "Where do we go next?"

3

EVOLUTION: WITHIN YOU AND WITHOUT YOU

Beware of greedy leaders
They'll take you where you should not go...
They just want to grow and grow,
Beware of darkness.
—GEORGE HARRISON

*I*n a fascinating, creative meditation, the channel inside me connects to the divine. My awareness of the moment expands beyond my five physical senses. My mind stops, and my heart opens to divinity and whatever it brings. I feel the peace in my body turn into a slowly intensifying bliss, sending ripples of energy to every part of me. My perception expands and I sense the oneness of life as well as separateness. Holding both of these perspectives simultaneously, I become aware that I am on a huge rock-like spaceship traveling through the galaxies.

I see millions of stars shining all around as I journey. I move ever onward and outward, like everything else in the universe. I am propelled by a rocket-like energy through the zero-point field of space. This energy pushing me is composed of all the accumulated light of the Sun. It is the history of Life on Earth. It is the collective experience of humanity and all its gathered information. It is the result of millions of interconnected, harmoniously integrated, functioning parts that apply information as fast as it is received. I feel it now as the wind in my sail.

I take a moment and feel it. I let my rock spaceship fly through the universe as I feel this power propelling me. I feel it in my body, my blood, my breathing, my DNA, and my molecules. I feel it stretching behind me back to the origins of time, and I feel infinite space accepting me as I fly forward through it. I hear a still small voice inside me say, "This is the experience of evolution. It is where you came from, where you are now, and where you are going. Take this moment to reflect. Consider that the collective human mind is more aware than ever; and that, in humanity, evolution is now conscious of itself."

My mind reels at the concept of evolution being conscious, I am just getting used to consciousness myself. I spend the rest of the meditation creatively imagining what evolution is and what it is conscious of. I keep coming back to a concept that all the knowledge humanity now holds is the only collective consciousness we know of. If evolution is conscious of itself right now, the only creatures that seem to know it are us. Is humanity's collective mind the result of the evolution of consciousness, or is humanity evolution's consciousness?

When we decided to go to the moon, a "critical path" emerged to get us there. In his book *Critical Path,* R. Buckminster Fuller discusses the process humans had to take—a path, which, from here to there, sometimes appeared impossible, and overwhelming. A proposed moon landing meant that scientists and engineers had to take thousands of years of accumulated knowledge, and then invent, discover, and create—through emerging technology—that much again or more collective knowledge—within just eight years. The brilliance of thousands of living scientists all over the world was funneled into the work, their efforts harnessed, coordinated, and collaboratively aligned in service to the goal.

The first manned moon landing was an international mass-media spectacular. Nothing like it had ever been seen on television, which was itself a still-fresh creation of human imagination. Millions of people around the world watched Neil Armstrong take that first step onto the surface of the moon, live and in real time. As a twenty-two-year-old hippie-visionary, I watched in awe and wonder as the miracle of television brought our collective human eye to witness the amazing feat. My nerves tingled in resonance with the rest of the world. In the aftermath of that sky-conquering event, a new perspective emerged, one that includes a bigger picture, and a dawning sense of oneness.

For the last fifty years, science has walked us toward the infinite in both directions, from the most microscopic to the most cosmic. Our collective eye is now able to see into atoms, even while it reaches past planets and galaxies several billion miles away. Human feet have walked the moon many more times, and some of our astronauts have returned to find their orbit in the halls of government.

Evolution itself is still a controversial notion, one that not so long ago got people who spoke about it hung. His evolutionary theories got de Chardin banned by the Roman Catholic Church. At the time, Church leaders did not accept Darwin's theory of evolution; it was viewed as heresy, diametrically opposed to the doctrine of creation. But Teilhard saw no conflict between evolution and Christian dogma. He taught that evolution always advances forward, primarily in a manner that integrates more and more complex structures geared toward consciousness. From atoms, molecules, and cells, he learned that a single thread of life runs through all. The principles that guide and rule the forces of evolution are just that: principles. All energy in the universe works according to certain principles. De Chardin believed that from the simplest to the most complex, these basic principles remain the same.

He proposed that humans are like cells forming a collective mind that will bring us together as one consciousness of humanity. He envisioned this occurring at a level far beyond anything possible to imagine; he viewed this as the purpose of evolution. He also proposed that humans had achieved "reflective" consciousness, a threshold that finds us becoming conscious of our awareness. Once evolution managed an upright cerebral cortex, standing tall and living in a different relationship with gravity, it could organize and store thoughts in the human brain. This organization of skills led to a capacity for mental reflection—the ability to review what had happened in the past, and conjecture as to how it might affect the future. This inward contemplative energy of reflective consciousness allowed humanity to develop communication, technology, and civilized society.

CHAPTER THREE

Evolution, reasoned de Chardin, does not appear to be evolving new forms beyond the human species. He believed that, in humanity, the force of evolution has found the limit of its outward reach, and now turns to "involution." He claimed that the human cerebral cortex is the end result of evolution's biological search for consciousness. Humans are evolution conscious of itself, and evolution conscious of the journey to discover itself. The next step, according to de Chardin, is on the inside—in the human mind and heart, in the realization of the soul, and in figuring out how to get along with each other.

De Chardin viewed the two World Wars as part of this development; he saw the patterns of socialization as going through transition and identity crisis. Various forms of socio-political philosophy were emerging in an attempt to fit the growing evolutionary sense of global unity: the "Super Man" of fascism, the self-organizing structures of capitalism, and the utopian ideals of communism.

Today, scientists turn their reflective consciousness to other areas of interest. Science has developed a method of tracking which part of the brain is being used during any thought or activity. They have discovered something rather peculiar in this undertaking: a specific part of the brain activates a sensor that perceives everything outside of the body as separate. For mystics and yogis to experience the high alpha states of oneness in meditation, this sense of being separate must be suspended. And so it is. Why? What is going on here? Serotonin, the hormone which accompanies these blissful states of oneness, rushes through the brain as we relax into the experience. What came first, the brain or the hormone? Do we think or meditate to release this serotonin, or does serotonin release to allow us to meditate? Science has discovered in studying these questions that what we focus our attention on has much to do with alpha state experiences.

Doctors also discovered, quite by accident, that another part of the brain, if removed or not present, causes a person to act without conscience. Certain patients with brain tumors who underwent surgery to remove the cancerous tissue had this specific part of the brain removed. Once released from the hospital, these folks acted as total strangers to the normal constraints of morality. They behaved without malice but thought nothing of lying, stealing, or murdering; this implies a biological basis for morality. Accumulated reports of cases like this were astounding to the medical profession, particularly when some patients actually grew back those parts of the brain that had not been totally removed.

Another interesting bit of evidence emerged when death row inmates were autopsied: this same portion of the brain was often missing. These findings led some to conjecture that perhaps criminality is not simply a behavioral issue, but is related to the biology of an individual brain.

Adding to the puzzle, modern life has seen the emergence of a multi-layered drug culture. From street drugs to prescriptions, we have spent a solid half-century overmedicating ourselves. Heroine, morphine, cocaine, speed, pot, alcohol, mood stabilizers, weight loss formulations, tranquillizers, sedatives, uppers, downers, numb-ers, and dumb-ers, are readily available, legally or otherwise, to anyone of any age. The war on drugs that has characterized our era is as official and martial as any combat situation overseas. The cost to society, in terms of mental illness, family breakdown, gang wars, and organized crime is staggering.

I return home after work, and surprise my longhaired musician friend of twenty years. He smiles sheepishly. He is sitting on his girlfriend's lap, trying to hide the fact that she is naked. They are sitting on the sofa in my living room. At first I don't notice the nudity; her long dark brown hair is covering her lanky shoulders and my friend is covering the rest of her. When he evades my questions, I begin to sense that something is up. In a moment it becomes obvious. The girl explodes with a leap, saying something unintelligible. She breaks free of my friend's grip and runs out the front door, naked, laughing like a little girl. He smiles at me apologetically and runs after her.

Later, I learn that this girl, who I will call "Dee," has been experimenting intensely with a number of different drugs — including peyote mushrooms and ecstasy — for the last month. She had gone to a reggae concert festival in Santa Barbara with another beautiful girl who had been encouraging a sexual liaison. The two women danced together like lusty sluts, publicly displaying their bodies at the concert. They attracted a group of drooling males who spiked the women's drinks with date-rape drugs and aphrodisiacs. Dee had "gone nuts" at the gig and was thrown out. She landed at my house because her boyfriend was working on a concert production with me.

All through the following week Dee had sudden, violent eruptions, often hurting herself or others. She needed constant supervision. Once everyone's nerves and resources were exhausted, we finally had to give up. We called for help and police arrived to take Dee to a mental hospital where she remained under treatment for two weeks. Once released, drowsy on psychiatric meds, she still behaved erratically. There was no noticeable improvement. Mentally, Dee was "out to lunch." The woman I'd known for four years was gone.

I was concerned for Dee not only because she was the girlfriend of a dear friend of mine, but also because I had often talked with her at productions I was involved in; we shared many intelligent and enlightening conversations, and I respected her youthful wisdom. My concern was over the possible mental, emotional, and physical harm she might have caused her body. My confusion was about how such a nice young lady, who was apparently very smart, could do this.

Drugs are chemicals, and chemicals are a major part of our physical being. Since much of our experience is dictated by biochemical interactions in the body, the use of drugs is serious business. Reckless drug use can lead to disastrous results, as happened with Dee. The body's hormones, endocrine glands, neural pathways and cellular receptor sites work together in an almost infinite variety of combinations to manage our biological existence. Biology influences emotional experience; chemicals are the key in the lock of our feeling states. In the complex modern world, emotional states can be triggered by rapid-fire inputs we barely even register on the conscious level. Once triggered, these states become highly personalized, especially if they are uncomfortable. We identify with the state—whether one of confusion, excitement, or depression—and imagine it to be who and what we are. But emotional states are far more fluid and changeable than we might think. Chemical interventions are a quick fix from outside of us that denies the latent power of the individual to steer the biochemical engine from the inside. In a world where chemical dependency—be it morning coffee or Prozac—is both common and acceptable, our latent human capacity for self-regulating our biochemistry remains largely untapped.

Every day, millions of people experiment with chemicals to change their emotional or physical experience. The dehumanizing environment of industrialized cities, the undermining and uprooting of family life, the increased frustration, violence, and sexual abuse common in our world; all these things push us to the limit, so we 'self-medicate' with drugs and alcohol. Self-medicating, with or without a doctor's supervision, is dangerous. Still, people risk death or madness daily; but to them, the risk is worth taking. They perceive their pain as unendurable, and believe they cannot function as responsible human beings without medication of some kind. Whether the problem is boredom, abuse, fatigue, or stress, our attitude toward chemicals is that they can answer the emotional need. Thus, we become dependent on drugs.

Who profits from the drug epidemic? The prison industries, the rehabilitation and urine testing industries, the chemical and pharmaceutical industries, and covert operations that get funding through smuggling and sales as well as arms trading—all profit from drug trade. These are all large power groups. Who pays? Taxpayers, prisoners, addicts; they pay in the form of taxes, legal fees, families, jobs, futures, and time in jail. The people who pay are treated as if they are insignificant—because the individuals preyed on by power groups are "nobody" compared to the huge, all-important motive behind the drug epidemic: profit.

Likewise, profit motives blind us when it comes to the environment. Our collective attitude toward chemical carbon emissions, which are the main cause of ozone depletion, the greenhouse effect, and global warming, is usually denial. For example, every year, millions of people travel to Las Vegas for a vacation-dream with lights, colors, and music everywhere. But very few of these folks are aware that the electricity fueling these lights, games, and entertainments in Las Vegas comes from the Hopi and Navajo sacred lands. The coal mines and power plants have desecrated the holy monuments of the Hopi and Dineh, dangerously depleted their water table, resulted in the forcible relocation of many Indian families, and added millions of tons of carbon emissions into the air—all for a gambler's dream.

And chemical terrorism—the threat of biological and germ warfare, anthrax, and napalm—represents another level of "better living through chemistry." Better living, in this case, is equivalent to eliminating the enemy. This may sound like a stretch, but the absurdity of the idea is only intended to highlight the absurdity of basic assumptions that go unexamined in a chemically-dependant world. When we transcend the brain function that mistakenly perceives itself as separate from everything, engineering our world through chemical use and abuse may become unnecessary. No longer will we be complicit while interests, such as tobacco, the pharmaceutical industry, and the oil-war machine, heap abuse onto the human body and the environment. The profit motive, "make money while you can, before anyone finds out how toxic the pleasure stick can be," so prevalent in a world where corporations have been granted the rights of persons, must be not only challenged but made obsolete. This can be done if we use the strength of our collective will to "Just say no" with our pocket books.

In 1980, R. Buckminster Fuller predicted that the digital communication industry would completely change our world. The Internet, e-commerce, and personal computers have brought that to pass. Bucky also believed that humanity's collective pool of knowledge, once made accessible and connected up by technology, would make it obvious that our political, economic, and social systems have become archaic because the principles those systems are founded on are no longer viable. Based on the premise that there is not enough for everyone and our tribe must compete to get their share, old systems are now being challenged. *Technology reveals that we do have the ability to feed, house, clothe, educate, and care for everyone on the planet if we use our resources wisely.* Clearly, the key is wisdom, and our survival may depend on how quickly we can collectively wise up. Old systems must transform. A *wise* populace is the best agent of change.

The inevitable change of the status quo is a major factor in the scramble for control of resources. Dealing with limited resources like petroleum means, economically, that whoever controls the last reserves cashes in on the last—gasp!—(and therefore biggest) profits. This perspective brings into focus the real reason for the Iraq war. In a last, desperate attempt to assert the old paradigm, neo-conservatives published a public paper entitled, *Rebuilding America's Defenses; Strategy, Forces and Resources for a New Century, A Report of The Project for the New American Century, September 2000*. The radical military-industrial complex reveals its true colors in this document, the result of a study conducted between Republican terms, while Clinton was president. The paper was published a few months before the Republican Party was reinstated in power in the 2000 Presidential election.

The 90-page paper[4] includes expert testimony by leading military industrialists blatantly outlining a plan for world domination by the United States. Claiming the need to maintain our current dominance for purposes of national security, the plan states that countries in the Middle East "like Iraq and Afghanistan" should be democratized by military force. The strategy also includes the democratization of Korea and other communist countries, with the United States establishing "a military presence" in all the major regions of the world.

Oil is crucial to the development of this plan. Arabian governments with their oil rich kings and fascist presidents (bullyboys like Saddam) are not the form of democracy supported by The Project. The form that profits the military-industrial complex and its corporations is the kind of democracy that makes cents for them.

The paper also puts forward an analysis of the American public, stating the people of this country would not back such a military offensive unless a catastrophe in the US "surpassing Pearl Harbor" were to stir up a supportive emotional climate for such a move. The paper was written and published before the catastrophe of September 11, 2001. Its existence, and the Bush administration's public acknowledgement of this paper as official policy, has fueled many a conspiracy theory.

Bannering this paper, the United States invaded Afghanistan and then Iraq. The Bush Administration has flaunted US military power to the United Nations and done its will with brash disregard for decades of worldwide agreements, armament treaties, and peace accords. The American military bullied its way into Iraq, took several months tracking

Saddam to his rat hole, and has now waged an illegal war in Iraq and the Middle East.

The evening news starts to look like a Fellini movie: John Wayne rides into town to clean up the bad guys because God, played by Charlton Heston, gave him the orders. As the movie ends, nothing is left of the town or the people who lived there; and we discover that John Wayne is a gay oil monger and Charlton Heston is the president of the National Rifle Association. Meanwhile, the European economy is slipping ahead of the United States, and with mad cow disease they have another excuse not to buy from us. They already don't like the arrogant bully president who ramrods the offensive, and now they begin to hate all Americans. Tourists from the US are assaulted and insulted, as well as having their tips thrown back at them, by Europeans.

Our collective human mind no longer accepts American foreign policy as representative of truly democratic principles. The United States is not the champion of democracy our leaders purport it to be. But the American way of life is still glorified, despite the cost to the rest of the world. Millions flock to the US to immigrate, legally or otherwise. The lure of television, fast cars, and credit cards is overwhelming. The poor, worldwide, look at American life and, understandably, want that life for themselves.

We want to have our cake and eat it too, so here we are, the supposed spearhead of evolution and the "crown of creation," trying to figure out how to get past the bully-phase and live the good life, how to not be homeless and destitute and left to die by the rich, how to get that Internet fix or that drug fix, how to get more sex, more money, more pleasure, more time, more, more, more. We might as well go ahead and admit it. People are not satisfied with what they have, they resist giving up what they've gained, and they want more.

Evolution is doing its work here and now, in our personal struggle to deal with these desires, the desire to have pleasure and avoid pain, the desire to amass material wealth and shun meaningful relationships, the desire to enjoy the majority of the world's resources while we are only a small fraction of the population. Evolution is you, here, thinking about pollution and the effect on future generations. It is you and I, even when we think we are victims of the universe, when we think we are the personality and the names we wear; we are really evolution moving through space-time.

Evolution discovers and invents us, allowing us to think whatever we want, giving us a gift of freedom: consciousness and willpower. Evolution has never been separate from God, but it is a modern way of defining God's ways. God is evolution, no less than everything else. The divine Creator set the course of creation as that of evolution. Since the beginning of time, evolution has faithfully run its course to finally manifest humanity, as it is now—semiconscious of divinity.

Within you, and without you, flows evolution. The strongest physical force in the universe—evolution—is the agent of life and the creator of consciousness. Evolution is who and what you are.

4

A Short History Of Human Tyranny

Just open your eyes, and realize, the way it's always been.
Just open your mind, and you will find, the way it's always been.
Just open your heart, and that's a start.
—The Moody Blues

Tyranny On The Outside

Every human is capable of murder and torture. The instinctive side of our nature is as real, and as invisible, as our bones. Human blood is spilled in the name of survival. Killing to survive is encoded in our DNA. Today denying this will not make it go away. In fact, denial empowers this side of our nature to stab us in the back, sabotaging society in a myriad of ways.

If civilization is a product of evolution's natural selection, perhaps the survival of the fittest now depends on humanity being able to control our bestiality.

Children learn this valuable lesson early, and first-hand. The sandbox is where I remember most of those initial confrontations. Placed there "to have fun playing with the other kids," while mom smoked and talked with her girl friends, I would tightly hold on to my brightly colored aluminum pail and shovel. But I would also eye the miniature dump truck and the shiny plastic dragon that squeaked, which the other kids in the sandbox had. If any of us acted out our aroused child's envy, we all discovered that the bullies who grabbed, hit, threw sand, or stole and ran were not much fun to "play" with. For the sake of social equilibrium, we are trained to control our impulses to kill, maim, or torture.

No one likes a bully; but, if we had our way, we would each choose to be the benevolent dictator/god. Children are born sensing that they are the center of the universe. For a period of time, developmentally, it is appropriate to feel like we are all there is. Eventually, mother becomes the first "other," and then comes the dawning shock that the body is separate from everything else.

As children we learn how to be clever instead of physically brutal, and we find sneaky ways to get what we want. When confronted by a playground bully, we might avoid physical confrontation in public, and then later call the bully names around the schoolyard. But the bully impulse goes much deeper than that. Abuse, whether physical, sexual, or verbal, of children, spouses, and others, is ingrained in family traditions and moral regulations. Our governments, churches, banks, and other corporate institutions run on the bully model of violent power abuse. Exploitation of others and violations of human rights are at the heart of profiteering and power-mongering.

Buckminster Fuller pointed out that the leaders of early human tribes were always the tallest men, because they could reach the fruit in the trees that others couldn't. That gave them power. When competing tribes intruded on a group's feeding area, the strongest and biggest men were on the front line. The smaller, cleverer guys figured out how to control the bigger ones through reward, punishment, and death. They got the bigger guys to fight other big guys and, eventually, the smaller, smarter guys maneuvered the tribe to go along with their ideas of how to live.

Then came the law of supply and demand, which was easy to exploit if you had a ship, could travel to find goods everyone wanted, could purchase them cheaply, bring them back to sell for top dollar, and do that repeatedly at both ends of a trade route. Buckminster Fuller called these men "pirates" and said that the methods pirates use have never really changed. They always use the most recent state-of-the-art technology to exploit the ignorance of others in order to amass great wealth and power for themselves.

Power structures evolved from this aspect of trade. At the heart of the matter lay a belief that killing other humans for profit is okay. In fact, the idea of murder is sanctioned by such power structures. All governments and most religions have used murder to get their way. Rudolf Steiner mentioned that the cult of murder was formed long ago in ages past, when some men agreed to murder their fellow human beings to maintain their position of power. This is domination and tyranny. But not all men agreed. Some would only kill if confronted with the threat of death or harm to their loved ones. Often, because they were so emotionally charged with righteous anger by the war propaganda that influenced their emotions to fight for the clever murderers, they would find themselves inflicting an extreme amount of violence, killing, or being killed. They would get played by the emotional heart-strings of religion, nationalism, genetic pride, fear, and greed. They found themselves exploited by the special interest groups' agendas, over and over again.

Make no mistake, at the heart of all political and economic institutions, the acceptance of murder as a means to an end is sanctified. The tribes, clans, and families of antiquity fought war after war. They fought invading, starving, and desperate foreigners, over and over again. When their own people suffered famine and drought, some of them would invade, kill, and steal in return. Then came the Scythian warriors in the seventh century B.C. who spread out from the plains of Asia on their horses to conquer the world. An additional list of world conquerors composed of such luminaries as Alexander the Great, Julius Caesar, Constantine, and Queen Victoria followed suit.

All this took humanity about 10,000 years before it came to a point where things began to change. That change was the most revolutionary time in Western history as monarchy after monarchy fell, and with them, the rolling heads of European government. When the ages-old noble class lost their status as rulers, the newly-rich, Industrial Revolution entrepreneurs stepped in. Humanity's agricultural energies were redirected. The industrial factory and city structure emerged.

During the last century, worldwide, 167-175 million "lives [were] deliberately extinguished by politically motivated carnage." War has cost the United States alone an estimated 560 trillion dollars since the American Revolution. This does not account for the emotional, psychological, environmental, and bodily damage to humans. The twentieth-century includes two great World Wars, touted as the "wars to end all wars." Those wars have demonstrated both the most hideous bullies and the most destructive weaponry in human history. Hitler, with his holocaust ovens, brought to bear on humanity a torture beyond the imagination of even the Inquisition. Then, finally, we saw the first atomic bombs deployed against an enemy country.

The generation to which I am born is the first in history to grow up with impending planetary doom hanging over our heads. This doom was, and is, part of our environment. Like television and cell phones, it is something we take for granted because it's there all the time. What is freaky about this is that it creates a very strange emotional experience, one of helpless resignation, deep within the psyche, where we can't quite get on with either living or dying. Like a death row inmate, we have a background sense that we are going to die any day, although it constantly gets put off for one reason or another.

The Inquisition and the Catholic Church did their best to exterminate every heretic and destroy every book or manuscript that refuted their power. They sanctioned and blessed the colonization of the heathen world by civilized Christians. They claimed the sole right and power to make kings. They controlled our information for centuries until we invented the printing press. The first book Guttenberg printed on his marvelous new invention in 1452 was the Bible, written in Latin. The Protestant revolution was the result. Kings kidnapped popes, and some even declared themselves pontiffs of their own religions. Torture and murder were commonplace. It became obvious to many people that war was once the way to make things right, but not any longer. Hordes of Utopian seekers left for the colonies to pioneer new ways.

As the colonial expansion and the exploitation of the world's resources grew, the cleverest of the European new-rich began to understand that they could be kings in their own new country. They had no problem just taking each country one at a time with murder, treachery, and tyranny. The greedier ones like Napoleon reached too far and were defeated. Others, like the United States, invested in war industries.

The DuPont family is a perfect example. They escaped France to save their heads in 1785, and began a gunpowder factory in the United States. Within a short time, they were providing gunpowder and dynamite to both sides of every war on the planet. Coupled as well with the cheap labor of the early Industrial Age and the American pioneers' needs for their products, the DuPont's became rich beyond what any kings in Europe had ever dreamed.

DuPont bought out General Motors in the early part of the 1900s with the help of the richest man in America at that time—Andrew Mellon, the Secretary of the US Treasury. Mellon not only was president of the country's biggest bank, the Mellon bank, but his company tapped the first oil gusher in the US and opened the first Petroleum gasoline station. Mellon heard that Ford and Diesel were planning to make their internal combustion vehicles with biomass fuels, rather than his petroleum-based fuels. The DuPont's assured Mellon that their cars would run on petroleum, and DuPont bought GM.

Around that same time, the British government formed the British Petroleum Company in order to exploit the oil in Arabia. By the 1920s, petroleum was the standard fuel for automobiles, and DuPont was building the first highways. Two specific phenomena brought staggering progress to the auto industry: assembly-line plants that could manufacture automobiles in mass quantities, and another new fangled invention: buying on credit.

The United States military jumped on the petroleum bandwagon and increased the use of this new fuel source from fueling trucks to developing tanks, planes, missiles, and bombs that also relied on petroleum. Good old Yankee ingenuity developed a huge and incredibly profitable war industry over the next several decades. By the end of World War II, every nation in Europe owed their entire economy to the US because of war debts. Since then, America has been involved in an endless stream of cold wars and hot skirmishes, becoming the leading military power in the world. One has to wonder—would war be so prevalent if it weren't so profitable?

Chapter Four

The connection between war and oil is undeniable. Our government has been involved, directly or indirectly, in hundreds of revolutions and wars across the globe. Terror and fear are basic facts of life in many parts of the world. And the war machine, which depends on oil, uses oil to assert its power across the globe.

Petroleum is now absolutely essential for any civilized country to compete in the world economy. Any emerging nation or third world country that wishes the luxuries of modern civilization must fuel it with oil. But petroleum is a limited resource. This petroleum fixation now threatens human civilization. At this rate, between the pollution and the wars caused by petroleum dependence, we face uncertainty as to how humanity is going to survive.

Tyranny on the Inside

Healthy anger is a survival mechanism that gives us extra energy and mobilizes action when we are threatened by danger. True anger is purposeful: it focuses on a problem and attacks it with all the power of the human being. Anger in this form is more animalistic than emotional. As an instinctive response, it is quite natural to feel angry when threatened. However, the emotional experience most of us identify as "being angry" is quite different and far less adaptive.

Civilization is a relatively new development in light of the millions of years it took our species to evolve. Despite the rapid rise of civilization, anger is still a jungle emotion. Human biology and biochemistry still influence our emotional state with primitive programs. Witness the fairly recent emergence of survivalist behavior in the modern-day jungle of our freeways: we call it "road rage." *Most of the time when we experience anger, there is no real immediate danger to our survival. Yet we feel our anger as though situations are a matter of life and death.*

In the absence of clear and present danger, our anger can get provoked when we feel oppressed or victimized by "the system" or by social or familial authorities. We begin to tell ourselves a story about how we are victims. We then build the pain and fear that results from that oppression into full-blown anger. As we grow and change, our anger likewise shifts its focus.

My anger toward my father transferred, almost without my noticing, onto the authoritarian practices of the government. Becoming an activist and speaking out for social and political change gave me a voice I did not have as my father's son.

While I was growing up, my father hit me if he felt like it, and thought nothing of it. The physical assault came hand in hand with verbal and emotional abuse—name-calling and cursing. To my father, this was "punishment," but I suspect that it was also frustration, impatience, and lack of skill. He had no experience dealing with children in any other way. He tried to condition me with fear, letting me know that he could and would punish me the moment I stepped out of line. As a result, I learned to be sneaky and plan my escape from his tyranny.

My father converted to Catholicism when I was five. Within that framework, I learned I was guilty, as were all human beings, due to original sin. The Church taught me to see myself as an unworthy sinner. I could be saved from the eternal torment of hell and damnation only if a threatening deity deemed me worthy of his mercy. A number of strings were attached to this mercy: church laws, rules of conduct, mortal as well as venial sins, penance, the Pope, and special rituals called "the sacraments." Were I to perform dutifully, and ask forgiveness for any transgression, my reward would be found in Heaven where I would, at last, be met with open arms by my creator. And if not, my punishment would be Hell and everlasting torture. The rite of Holy Communion, wherein a piece of bread is "transubstantiated" into God's body and placed in the mouths of the faithful, was the only reward to be expected in this life.

Catholicism introduced yet another layer of authority in my life. Nuns and priests were to be respected and feared just like my dad. They, too, exercised power in the form of threats and actual physical punishment. The face of one particular redheaded priest is forever burned into my memory. I can still see his bright red countenance and the look of outraged disbelief that made him pout and squint his eyes as he beat the switching stick against his palm. When he whacked the top of my wooden desk with the switch, he said, "There are two motivating forces in the universe, love and fear; if you won't learn for love, by God, you'll learn through fear!"

CHAPTER FOUR

It is 1963. I am eighteen, and a senior in a Catholic high school.
It is not quite a year since the assassination of JFK, and the Beatles
have just hit #1 on the billboard charts for a historically unprecedented
28th week in a row. I have let my bangs grow long like Paul
McCartney and Ringo Starr. I am dating a new girl who likes my
curly mop top. After school one autumn day, the testosterone pumps
through my pubescent body as we walk hand in hand down the street to
the gym. We make plans to get together after football practice and I go
to change into my uniform. A group of guys on the team ambush me
at practice. The coach and the principal look the other way when I am
forced to the ground. I begin to struggle, but realize that I alone cannot
stop the mob. The gang energy terrifies me; the scissors could slip and
seriously hurt me if I try to fight them off, so I submit. My rage and
anger go undercover, but later I say and do anything I can to shame
those boys. I hate them for humiliating me, and I hate the priests and
nuns who have allowed this to happen.

Before long, I turn to alcohol, more for the strength it gives me
than for solace. But inexperience leads me to overdo it, and I get drunk
at school one day. I am suspended from twelfth grade for being drunk
in class. When I get home that afternoon, my parents are sitting in
the living room with a couple from the parish. Everyone seems very
upset. I hear my mother wailing, my father moans, "Where did we go
wrong? Where did we go wrong? What did we do to deserve this?"

Looking back, I see that my parents' behavior set a template that
impressed on me a specific pattern of blame. The emotional energy of the
victim is very convincing, and the pattern of feeling victimized is seductive.
I fell under the spell of it instantly, and saw that I could blame everything
on everyone else. I learned to deal with my anger by wailing, moaning,
complaining and blaming. I used my anger as a switch of punishment. In
the school of hard knocks, I learned to "take it"—take abuse, that is—and
righteously turn it around and in turn, abuse others. Ever since those first
clear lessons, I have practiced and mastered the art of blaming others for
my frustration just as my parents did.

When my body grew into that of a young man at age eighteen,
I finally stood up to my dad. It is a passage every boy of an oppressive

father remembers. On that special day in 1963, my dad lost his temper and began to yell at me. He put his hands on me in a threatening manner and I responded immediately, shoving him away with all my force of will and a young man's growing strength. I looked him in the eye and said, "Don't you ever touch me like that again!" He never did.

Determined not to be like my father, I adopted a peaceful, happy-go-lucky, nice-guy personality. I was never violent, never angry, and always kept a positive, smiling attitude. I fell in love with my façade and became deeply identified with it in every way. In fact, I actually believed it was me; that is, until my kids became teenagers.

An early evening in 1992 and I have just had a very tough day at work. I am exhausted, feeling slightly grumpy, under so much stress I can barely keep my mellow going. I'm looking forward to a toke when I get home to ease the physical and emotional stress. I am glad to be off work, and glad to be home. As I open the door, pandemonium greets me. The noise is deafening; three kids trade off yelling at a fourth, who is screaming. I feel a surge of energy; repulsion mixes with meanness and blind-sides me. Suddenly, a huge wave of irritable, angry impatience crashes over me and I begin to rage. My mind intervenes, and somehow I stop myself, trying to think of a way to control this situation before someone gets hurt.

One of the kids hurls a cutting, angry threat at the smaller one and makes a move toward him. I see his violent intention and explode. Words rush up through me like a volcano, and I hear myself scream at the top of my lungs. The emotional force and physical vehemence of my reaction sears my vocal cords, I am completely hoarse in less than a minute. I am literally rendered speechless, unable to say another word. Exasperated, I pick up an empty coffee cup, and hurl it in my son's direction, intending to miss him. On impact, the cup smashes into pieces and leaves a dent in the wall. I stand there, shocked. I look at my son and recognize his expression—I remember looking at my dad with the very same expression on my face. My son struggles to hide the fear, shame, and rage he feels. He looks me in the eye, and lets me know with a glare that I will not destroy him. Not a word is spoken.

CHAPTER FOUR

That incident occurred over twelve years ago, and yet I am still haunted by it. I had sworn I would not be like my dad, but I lost it—and there I was, an exact replica. The similarity was simply too obvious to deny. I tried to clear the air with my son; someday, I believe, we will totally heal that experience. Meanwhile, I meditate on it constantly, because the action of throwing that cup woke me up. I could no longer pretend I did not have a problem handling my anger.

At first, I once again fell prey to feeling like a victim. I tried to convince myself that it wasn't my fault and blamed my father, rationalizing that I had somehow inherited his anger. Several years would pass before I could fully accept and face what was inside me. Meanwhile, anger came up in me more and more, and I stuffed it, along with my shame, into my denial drawer. No one was protected—my kids, my wife, my friends, my teachers, my boss—anyone could be the target for my rage. The stronger my anger became, the more I bottled it up inside.

Then I fell in love with a girl half my age. In her, I found someone to butt heads with, until the relationship began to resemble a head-on collision. We were two of a kind; both of us were chips off the dark-side-of-the-abuse block. That girl could push my buttons—and then some. Not until my love for her turned to hatred and my thoughts blurred with imaginings of murder and suicide, did I recognize that I was out of control. My denial finally broke down. The pain and agony of those years marked the start of my healing.

> *I have reached the point of standing with my hand on the oven gas knob, ready to take her sleeping body and my own out of this life. In this moment I suddenly realize that I have to change or my rage will destroy me. I vow to get to the root of the pain—I never want to feel this way about a loved one again. I realize that murder or suicide is not the answer; there must be a better way to deal with my anger. I need to look for help.*

That was when I discovered I was co-dependent, and I consciously began a recovery program to heal myself. I laughed when the books I read said it takes four years or more. I thought I could beat that easy in one or two. It took six. I never went to Twelve Step programs because I do not agree with their external concept of God. But I did read all the best teachers in the recovery field and I put together an organically evolving recovery program that includes therapy sessions and a focus on taking responsibility for my own experience.

Along the way, the world at large began to look different. What I had always seen as an issue of authority, the power-control trip that seems to permeate our entire society, the constant push and pull of dominate or be dominated, instead revealed itself as a struggle in the heart of each and every human. When motivated by anger, we want to destroy and eliminate what we perceive as the source of discomfort. We think up and plan destructive actions. This is our survivalist, "jungle" behavior rearing its me-or-you primitive head. My jungle-thinking told me it was a moral obligation to protect other males from this girl—to make sure none of my brothers would have their heart and head scrambled too. I wanted to believe it was my responsibility to do something to eliminate her rather than allow future human sorrow. I can laugh at it now, but the thoughts were most convincing at the time.

Arrogance hardly describes this form of thinking, but I have no better word (save perhaps "psychotic") for the strange idea that I have the clarity to determine who should live or die. As a thought process, whether engaged in by an individual or a government, this is quite suspect. Some imagine they can and should do it, and are full of righteousness as they determine who shall live and who shall die; but the human collective jury is still out.

I watched the Nuremberg trials on television when I was a kid, and the 1961 movie with Spencer Tracy called "The Judgment At Nuremberg." Some Nazi soldiers were convinced that "just following orders and doing their job" was an acceptable excuse for aiding tyranny and murder. Many others, mostly Jews upset about the Holocaust, believed that this was not acceptable. As a youngster being raised in America's democracy, I felt a rebellion against any authority that would burn or gas innocent people. I enjoyed hearing the news stories of how the war criminals were tracked down, held prisoner, and put on trial. Most of all I loved the real-life drama of the court and its justice, which dared to put these men on trial and made them account for their actions. I was not aware that my conscience was evolving as I watched, but now I realize that those Nuremberg Trial broadcasts impressed me with values that my Catholic catechism could not even get close to.

Never before those trials had there ever been any expression by the collective human mind as to what is unacceptable in war. Now, someone was actually saying, on TV and to the world, that tyrannical murder—the kind that seeks to eliminate an entire race—is unacceptable. Even more importantly, the point was made, graphically, that a soldier *must* question and disobey orders when the orders are unreasonably prejudiced and target certain groups for extermination.

Tyranny of all kinds, and war most obviously, seeks to eliminate the people we have become prejudiced toward, whether out of fear from a *perceived* threat, or from an *actual* threat. On a personal level, our behavior toward our families and loved ones is equally focused on this same energy of tyranny, seeking to eliminate the behavior in them that we don't like. We don't like who they are or what they do, and we seek to force them to become who we think they should be. The challenge, which we face with family and loved ones when we cannot accept them as they are, is the same challenge the countries of the world face when it comes to accepting each other. It has the same dynamics, same principles, same values, same attitudes, same control and power issues. And when push comes to shove, whether at home or in the world, the remedy that leads to peace is always the same: tolerance and respect for diversity.

5

POWER UP, POWER DOWN, POWER ALL AROUND

Reach out your hand if your cup be empty
If your cup is full may it be again
Let it be known there is a fountain
That was not made by the hands of men
—JERRY GARCIA AND ROBERT HUNTER

The word "power" *sounds* powerful. It conjures up many images and associations in the mind—from battery power to nuclear power, and from personal power to the power of God. We often speak about "having" power as if the ultimate goal in life is to possess and command as much of it as possible. But another kind of power exists, a power that cannot be commanded, possessed, or stored up for later use. This kind of power, once discovered, is a resource that constantly renews itself, and ensures we will never suffer depletion. It is the power of inner freedom and choice.

In his book, *Seat of the Soul* (Simon & Schuster, 1990), Gary Zukav highlights the difference between "external power" and "authentic power." He defines external power as anything outside of us that we impose on others. Authentic power, on the other hand, is within; it is our intrinsic connection to the real power of creation, life, and eternal spirit.

Civilization has its roots in the use of external power. Since men first began to invent and use tools, we have exercised external power over the natural world. Each progressive age—from the Iron Age through the

Agriculture, Industrial, and Technology Ages—the use of external power has allowed humanity to head steadily in the direction of "progress." This progress has led us to the point where nuclear power and the proliferation of nuclear weapons could obliterate all life on Earth. *The archaically designed systems that currently hold the world's power control the largest state-of-the-art external power system ever created.* We value this external power precisely because we wield it against any power that threatens us. The problem is that external power often turns on us, because as Newton's third law states: "Every action has an equal and opposite reaction." Nuclear power is a clear example. We split the atom and, in so doing, acquire the means by which to bring about mass extinction. Training terrorists, who later terrorize us, is another example of how this power eventually is used against us.

How did we get here? And, more importantly, now that we are here, how do we turn the power equation around? How do we tap the resource of authentic power within us and apply it to the imbalance of power being expressed in our world?

Let's begin at home—where the power differential often first arises—between a child and his or her parents. I grew up during a time when parents often treated children in a violent, abusive manner. Some of my earliest experiences, and those of many men and women of my generation, involved the external power of angry adults. Yelling in anger, calling names, insulting in public, threatening physical harm, slapping, kicking, or using "the strap"—were quite common. Ours was not a generation that had the benefit of conscious parenting, which is why Dr. Spock's books on healthy childrearing became so popular with our parents—they were seeking information that had not been publicly available until then. My father thought nothing of calling me "worthless," "no good," or "stupid." I can still hear his voice in my head saying, "Who do you think you are, King Shit?" Much of what was considered normal just forty years ago, such as "spare the rod, spoil the child,"[6] is now considered child abuse, and is a criminal offense. Why does any parent think there is nothing odd with treating and talking to children in a violently abusive manner? In our human past it has been our path to talk to children, and treat children, like dogs. In a truly civilized world there is no abuse of children, and we may yet attain such a civilization if we but look at our children with respect—respect for the divinity and humanity flowing through them, respect for life and the future that children are, and respect for the healing of humanity's collective inner child.

The collective pain from abuse cannot be addressed with more external power. Fortunately, healing does not depend on external power. Healing comes from the eternal and transcends space and time. Just for a moment, center your attention fully on this: what is the feeling of the collective human misery from abuse? There is tremendous power in feeling that collective pain. Can you feel it? Opening the heart to experience that collective pain is perhaps the greatest catalyst for authentic healing. *Feeling the collective human experience of abuse, even for a second, initiates a process by which each person begins to effectively heal that pain for the whole. This is the beginning of authentic power.*

To be part of the solution, we must fully embrace the problem. The following exercise is helpful for accessing authentic power.

> *Sit quietly for a few minutes. Begin to direct your attention, your thoughts and prayers, toward those on this planet who are directly suffering from abuse. With all the love you can feel in your heart, and all the love you can visualize in your mind, direct your heart and channel love toward those suffering from abuse. Love them as deeply and completely as you possibly can, giving all you have, to this moment of active care and concern.*

This exercise allows us to both connect with, and generate, inner power. Love is the door to this power, and focus is the key that allows us to open that door.

External power is distorted, even false, because it appears to work—or at least get the job done—but it has no heart and does not endure. The difference between fake power and real power comes down to this question: does it endure? Authentic power connects with the source of abuse within our self and responds with the true power of love, thus transforming our heart and enabling it to endure enough to help many others heal as well. The human heart, once opened, is a source of limitless power.

CHAPTER FIVE

"Love" is the word we use for this feeling of opening up our heart and for the very serious endeavor of healing. This is not the kind of love we have for hamburgers and flashy clothes. Love is the energy of the universe, but more than that, it is who we are. We are love incarnate; we always have been and always will be. We are eternally changing, not out of boredom, or fear, or lust; but changing to become a higher expression of life, which is love. Life can be a dismal experience if we think it is and keep the heart closed. But even pain is transformed into a beautiful and fulfilling experience when we reach for the higher and nobler parts of the Self and find divinity in every form we meet.

If we believe what we see on the news night after night, the world can look like it is evolving toward bully-domination. But we can, with sharper focus, see a world that is also evolving out of the bully stage and into something entirely new. The principles of duality help us understand the activation of energy, and it is in energy that we find the real definition of power. Power is either moving or stored energy, but always energy. Without energy, there is no power. Energy can destroy or create; it can be generated, transmitted, controlled, focused, transformed, and transduced. Without something to relate it to, energy or power is meaningless. What good is having a billion tons of oil if no one wants it? The more people want something we have, the more power we have—but the more power we must also exert to keep it.

Within each of us is a mechanism that senses power in much the same way we sense gravity, attraction, and the potential collision of bodies and wills. This mechanism, or innate capacity, also senses the dualities of life. For the physical universe to function, the law of duality remains constant. Duality is like a magnet with polarity: at one end, energy comes in, from the other end, energy flows out. Two input poles will repel each other, as will two output poles. An in and an out will attract magnetically and stick together, allowing a unidirectional current through them both.

In the realm of atoms, we find that these dualities of positive and negative polarities have relationships that create molecular structures with other atoms. From the molecules, cells are created, and from the cells, bodies are grown. From bodies come families, tribes, nations, civilizations, and technologies. Atoms and cells have been involved throughout the evolution of Nature. The fallacy of humanity's use of external power is obvious: humans have been acting as if they are separate and different from Nature. Humans act as if they believe they can live without Nature's environment and survive. Humans separate themselves from Nature and attempt to conquer it. But, humans are not separate from Nature—we come from Nature, as well as being nourished and sustained by the natural world.

In the Pathwork Guide lectures, Eva Pierrakos identifies our attitude about this: "The forcing-current says, 'you must,' and you make demands on others to be, feel, and do what you need and desire."[7] The term "forcing current" describes a specific type of power that is available to all humans at all times. Like electricity, the forcing current is always there, waiting for us to plug into it. We can feel its force when we use it, or when it is used on us. When we want something, we must exert energy to change or manipulate circumstances to achieve our ends. Our attitudes affect our choice of strategies; how we see the desired object, or perceive its value, determines the intensity of our efforts to discover all the options to help us achieve it.

As human animals, we are familiar, although sometimes unconsciously, with our bestial ancestry showing its fangs. Everywhere we look, we see examples of how to wield the forcing current. Some of the most barbaric are also the most applauded. In addition to blatant bloodshed, certain facial expressions, words, and gestures typify our use of the forcing current. The immense popularity of movie and video game heroes attests to the archetypal and universal appeal of what we can also simply call aggression. We make heroes of the strongmen who protect themselves and others from the bullies. They are quick to cripple and kill those who threaten innocent people. Often, these heroes cross the fine line of protection into the area of punishment. That is when we see them do illegal things to deal out justice in their own way. "Sometimes you just have to kill 'em," is the bottom line rationalization.

Of course, everyone can think of some situation in which his or her loved ones were threatened seriously. All of us would face the attacker and try to kill them rather than be killed. By extrapolation, we are brainwashed into following the cattle calls used by the slaughterhouse workers: "To protect your children, families, homes, your way of life, and your lives, we must go to war. Come this way; some of you may die, but the enemy will be vanquished and your death will be one of honor. Come on now, let's get over this threatening catastrophe and back to business as usual."

The forcing current, whether expressed by an oppressive government or our own ego, will use all tools available to manipulate us. Sex, money, rewards, punishments, ego-inflation: all serve as a carrot out in front of the ass to get that loaded wagon pulled for someone else's agenda. Men are dragged out in front of a firing squad, have their assets confiscated, wives raped, children turned against them—all through the use of forcing current. I can yell at my lover to get my way, or I can act seductively and flirt. Both are expressions of the same forcing current.

Authentic power, on the other hand, has as its base the intention to respect others. It can be seductive, playful, and fun; but always takes the needs of the other into consideration. Authentic power does not seek to dominate; it seeks to connect and bridge. Authentic power enables us to be our real self and accepts and engages the real self of others. It is concerned with "our" agenda—your agenda and my agenda—equally.

Anger in response to a scene that does not involve an immediate physical threat imposes a life-or-death context on the situation. This puts the forcing current to use in a way that may serve the short-term goal of getting what we want, but often results in long-term ill effects. Spouting off in a rage whenever we don't get our way is a sure sign we have fallen into a "dominate or be dominated" mode. Consider that you already know very well how to use the forcing current with anger or otherwise, even whether you use it or not. Consider also that you are aware of most of the forcing modes available. Television and movies give us a thorough education on this. But we are collectively less aware of non-forcing modes. Alternatives to anger are an acquired skill for most of us. And, like any new skill, these new modes come with the frustrating failures we experience along any learning curve.

Power Up, Power Down, Power All Around

Since 1980, the Non Violent Communication Foundation has advanced a system of compassionate communication models developed by Marshall B. Rosenberg, Ph.D. As a resource, Non Violent Communication (NVC) can help us define our experience, define our feelings, and define our needs. The process teaches strategies that work in terms of getting our needs met while helping us feel better and build relationships. This simple process uses no external power or forcing energy whatsoever. Rather, it teaches how to open to another human and really listen to their feelings and honestly communicate our own.

NVC is a system that recognizes the tricks that get anger escalating into violence, and the tricks that lead to co-dependent abuse, and how to avoid those traps. NVC recognizes how certain words trigger a negative polarity response and how to avoid using them or being affected by them. It is considered by many experts to be the most powerful communication development of the modern age. Trained NVC facilitators now are called in to perform conflict resolution in some of the most volatile places on Earth.

Let us consider another important resource for authentic empowerment, the concept of "choice point." Choice point teaches us to recognize that there are certain points in life when our choices are extremely important. These are the choices that could affect our future in a really big, adverse way, or in a very positive and empowering way. These choice points may occur in one person's life only a dozen times, or hundreds. We often only see through hindsight when and where our choice points were. But the power in choice points comes with recognizing them when they are happening.

Paying attention to intuitive signals helps us identify choice points. These feelings usually try to get us to recognize something we aren't aware of, like the real potential consequences of our choices. The most important choice points seem to be the ones where our life will be dramatically changed. How many of the big choice points in your life were you aware of at the time they happened, and aware of all the consequences, and aware of all the choices?

CHAPTER FIVE

Which brings us to the choice points of our inner child. Many crucial choice points are affected by the attitudes we developed in choices we made as a child. These are the choice points we most suffer from, because our inner child uses the power of those early choices to make our adult life uncomfortable. It is precisely these decisions, hidden deep in the unconscious, that need to be exposed to our awareness if they are to loosen their hold on us. Finding these memories sometimes takes professional help, but through honest self-reflection and effort, most people can gain access to the inner child aspects of the self where life-shaping decisions are held.

When we take responsibility for our inner child, and begin the process of reflecting whenever we sense its childish influence; then the child will show us how our attitudes toward sex, women, men, money, or anger were all formed in our personality back in childhood. This is really the most valuable work for anyone on the path to his or her higher self. When we can remove the obstacles of the past that keep us from being who we really are, our authentic selves become accessible to us.

The ultimate power of all, omnipresence, exists in the eternal now of this moment. This power is the true source of all things; it is the center of centers. It always has been. It exists everywhere in all dimensions, directions, forms, and energies. It is equally accessible from anywhere in the universe by all existence.

The power of omnipresence concentrically flows through all things. Evolution and life thrust through separation to union, holding the reality of unity and oneness, yet allowing the freewill diversity of expression and experience to manifest. This is the eternal moment of omnipresence: always here and now, with all of time parading through, all the temporary forms living and dying, and all the possible variations of light, life, and love.

This power has been neglected because of our fixation on external power. No external power anywhere in the universe is eternal, only the omnipresence always here and now is eternal. Only authentic power, power from inside each individual self, can touch this eternal omnipresence with awareness. When we do this, we touch our eternal

Self. We are omnipresence, everyone is; but most of us are only aware of our personality, attached to the body which we have this lifetime. When we identify with the body, we do not acknowledge or experience our larger existence outside the body; therefore the source of most of our fears is the fear of non-existence, or death.

What is this body? What part of it does not come from the Earth and the sun? Where does it start, with the food of today, and air I breathe now, or yesterday? And who is experiencing this body? When the body dies, where is the experiencer?

In 1895, Ramana Maharshi "died" at sixteen—then lived to be eighty-five wearing little more than a loincloth. At age eighteen, he entered a blissful state and did not communicate verbally for nine years. The energy emanating from Ramana was so powerful that people flocked from all over the world to sit near him. When he finally broke his silence, it was to speak of the power he had connected with when he asked the question, "Who am I?" He said it was revealed to him that he was not the body that dies, but the eternal omnipresent spirit experiencing the body. Through rigorous truthful inquiry he was able to discover his real self.

Ramana spent the rest of his life helping others experience this larger Self. Thousands made pilgrimages to see him every year. The peace, stillness, and love felt in his presence changed people, and opened their hearts and minds to the timeless truth of Self-realization. The power of Ramana's personal presence was famous and legendary. Of course, some who went to see him did not understand, they wanted to make him give them the type of power he had. Those people missed the value of his teaching.

The ultimate choice is yours. Do you want the power you are? Do you feel and live what you think you know? Or are you a powerless victim of the universe? What is important to you about power? If you want true power and can't find it, look around; it is everywhere. Access to it is available now through bookstores, the Internet, teachers, workshops, meditation, and in your talents.

CHAPTER FIVE

To empower yourself means to recognize that the power does not come from external things or energies, it comes from inside you. External things have a limited and very temporary power. Inside you is more power than all the external power there ever was or will be. This is why true freedom, the personal quality we identify as "nobility," and the democratic process have survived in spite of tyranny or oppression. The power of murder ends with death. The power of a liberated soul lives on and on, past the death of the body. The power of evolution flows ever onward. The words of martyrs and heroes have inspired us long after they are gone, words that speak chillingly of truth and life in the face of death. Freedom? Where did the word come from, but from those who inspired us to throw off the yoke of oppression and liberate our spirits?

Yet, as in the case of ignorance in the presence of an enlightened master, it is the power of ignorance that keeps us from seeing what is right in front of our face. Ignoring reality has tremendous power and sustains the denial of truth. The difference between reality and truth is slim. Reality exists relative to each individual perspective. Truth is eternally true for all. Many people are intent on piling up more ignoring on top of the ignorance, which never solves anything. Truth is what endures, and it is what liberates us from ignorance.

Ignorance stems from ignoring truth. Ignorance looks away from the eternal present moment, the eternal nature of our self, the connection with that source of eternal love that sustains all temporary things and experiences. It ignores the connection of unity and oneness. And it ignores higher perceptions: multidimensional awareness, intuitions, insights, and imagination. Ignorance is a choice; every human has the ability to choose to wallow in it; or they can choose, and eventually must choose for the evolution and salvation of their own soul, to experience truth.

Ignorance has no feeling; it is numb, innocent, and naive. Truth is felt to the core of the experience, to the heart and soul of the being, destroying all illusion. Truth eventually reveals the eternal omnipresence of divinity.

We are horrified at the atrocities of war because we deeply feel these atrocities are against the truth of oneness and unity, the truth we actually are. When we choose to use external power in reaction to war, we are acting out of ignorance. Ignoring the truth, we end up being just another bully fighting the old bully.

The real power is in change. The I Ching is based upon this premise: "The only constant in the universe is change." The power to change, which exists in humans, is exponentially beyond that of any other entity we have discovered. Humans stay stuck, and not changing, through ignoring truth. Because the pope said that God said that the Earth is the center of the universe, people were murdered for saying, "The Earth is orbiting the sun." However, change takes being willing to use our resources, considering as many options as we can, developing strategies to meet our goals, and adapting.

Consider how many resources you use when you change. What resources do you remember using during important changes of your life? Can you recognize the resources you ignored back then? What about options? Remember how many times you listed the options as one or two, and then found out later that there were dozens of options you never considered? Do you really research your available options? Do you use the same old ineffective strategies that get nowhere but to frustration? What about goals? Can you even define your goals clearly to yourself? What do you want the changes in your life to feel like? What strategies would help that?

Most folks are too overwhelmed by the vast variety of choices involved in change, so they only change through the external power patterning. They change because of the manipulations and pressures of parents, teachers, friends, businesses, governments, and religions. They go along with these influences in order to avoid being socially rejected—but behind closed doors they rebel.

To change ourselves, taking full responsibility for our experience and using our own inner authentic power, is the only enduring and consensual choice. It is in consensus with all our parts: our personality, heart, and spirit. It endures because those choices we take responsibility for are embraced by our heart and will.

Like the humble hobbits, we must destroy the ring of fear that binds us to systems of darkness, for fear is the only source of their external power. Fear is the heartbeat of war. Fear is the rush hour traffic paying their bills. Fear is abandonment and rejection. Fear is anger at what was done and believing it will be done again. Fear is a blinding influence that calls on the awesome power of self-rejection, which forces us to endure abuse upon abuse. Fear is destroyed only by relentless use of the authentic power within us, which knows we exist past death and all changes.

So the final battle is here. You are facing yourself and your fears. Realizing that you fear only yourself, you leave the front lines of the heroic carnage where the forces of Light are meeting the hordes of Darkness and their minions. You rush to the darkest places within yourself and find the source of this violent, evil power. There you choose to disempower it forever by taking responsibility to be true, and free, and to act with awareness. Now imagine that there are millions of people also doing the same thing. Picture the change, as you and these people embrace the nobility of the human experience and open your heart to all the rest of humanity and the Earth. Can you feel the bigger change you are a part of? Evolution, the swell of the tidal wave, is the tsunami of human consciousness you partake in and are.

It is 1995 and my world seems to have come to an end. My girlfriend has just dumped me and I am crazy with anger and frustration. I am penniless, living on the street, and trying to piece my mind and heart back together. My insides feel like Mount Saint Helens, bursting with fire and explosive rage. I swing between thunderous curses against everything I see and torrents of fiery tears that burn through my soul. I have never felt so desperate. I can hardly contain the conflicting energies: sorrow, pain, regret, and remorse.

I consider suicide, convinced that I cannot tolerate these painful feelings much longer. I sit in disgust, angry with a silent god who seems not to notice my prayers at all; I wail at him for causing this to happen. Everything I thought I knew is meaningless. I am totally alone. I've been rejected by my family and friends, and have no one to whom I can turn. I have no choice but to go inside myself. I sit down and start thinking, "What do I know for sure about life?"

Power Up, Power Down, Power All Around

All I can come up with is this: 1) we all die in the end, and 2) we can't live without air. I try to hold my breath. The air eventually escapes against my will. I blow it all out and try to keep it from coming in, but my body throws me aside as it gasps for air, asserting its will over my strangely deranged mind. I begin to contemplate the mystery of breath. Sensing the need to calm myself, I lapse into a meditative style of breathing. Slow in, slow out, full, deep, slow breaths. I can feel my body begin to relax, and yet the thoughts are still relentless. I begin to focus, directing my mind toward things that bring comfort. I center my mind on God, the Divine Mother, the love that permeates all things and threads in and throughout life. Slowly, these thoughts take root and become prominent in my awareness.

Eventually, I center myself enough to accept and know that I have what I need for the moment. I reflect on how much breath and meditation practices are my treasured tools that work and are worth the time and effort. I feel calmed and refreshed in the knowing that breath is my connection, my portal into my body, and the bellows that flames my emotional experience — which only I can calm through my breathing. Then, healing love comes in a wave and I feel the ability to comfort myself. From here, I can embrace my sorrow. The suffering is soothed, I calm down, and healing begins.

Healing from the intense emotional confusion of that period took several years, but my breathing and meditation practices helped me find that calm center in the eye of my hurricane. I learned to ride that core of white light all the way up by being still, peaceful, and unwavering in meditation. Focused breathing and meditation linked me up with authentic powers of peace, love, truth, trust, and acceptance—without which I would be dead or insane. These powers, which I only turned to as a last resort, are now my saving grace. They give my will strength and my vision clarity. They are my right and left hands; I am never without them. Breath and stillness are my constant companions—always available.

In fact, meditation is much, much more than sitting still. That is how meditation starts, but eventually, that stillness becomes a state of mind. Meditation is focused attention that keeps a steady stream of awareness on the Self—not in the ego sense, but in the essence sense—and sees that higher Self everywhere, in every being. Meditation is right mindfulness, keeping the mind harnessed. When left to itself, the mind is the biggest tyrant of all. Willing to do anything to whip us into a bucking-bronco frenzy over what it imagines is real, the mind constantly runs wild. The tyranny of our mind would have us think its worrisome sidetracking thoughts are all-important. Meditation is the gate to freedom from this mental slavery.

There are many, many ways to enter into the practice of meditation. Most start with an intentional focus on breath, a sound (mantra), or a prayer. My practice starts with a focus on breath. In the tradition of Ramana, I then ask the question, "Who am I?" and accept all that comes.

Breathing in a centered manner opens you to all that is, accepting whatever arises as the Self. You then wield all forms of power with authentic power. Every form of power mentioned here is in you. Actually, you are the source of all these powers. The more you know this, and accept it, and use it, the more empowered you are.

Cultivate true power with patience and you will reap the harvest of power as the experience of your Self—manifesting in truth, freedom, and love. For this is power, our human power: to take all that humanity gives, and to go within our individual experiences to eventually give back what we have learned to the whole. Our greatest power as humans is to *be individual and unified at the same time.* For that is the power of our being, our true Self: to hold the polarities in both hands: *to know individual experience, and at the same time, to be aware of our unity in omnipresence.*

This is the power that can, as John Lennon said, "Imagine there's no countries." This is the power Martin Luther spoke of when he said, "I have a dream." Like Isaiah, the Old Testament visionary, King saw that, "The glory of the Lord shall be revealed, and all flesh shall see it." For truly, the power of evolution is consciousness itself, and every human has the potential to consciously evolve. We are the next step on the ladder. Evolution has become conscious of itself in humanity. Embrace this power we are, it is within your reach. It is in your blood and bones. It is you. You are the power, so be it.

6

THE JUDGE

Long lost brother of mine
Walking the dream evolution...
Long lost brother of mine
Seeing my life for the first time
—ANDERSON, BRUFORD, WAKEMAN AND HOWE

I t is December 1998, four years have passed since my wife and
I split up. I am bothered by the fact that my children live fifty
miles away. The situation feels unnatural, I want to see my
kids more, but dare not insist. Learning to manage my anger
has become a priority and I am seeing a therapist to help me get
a grip. She uses a specialized rapid-eye movement approach called
EMDR. The process is relatively simple; I follow the tip of her waving
pencil with my eyes and keep my head still. She directs me to focus
inwardly on memories and re-experience the events that brought on
angry reactions while the eye-movement process is happening. After
a few minutes, she tells me to relax and pay attention to how I feel.
Then, we repeat the sequence again.

I feel very psychedelic, in an altered state. My emotions are
definitely shifting as the internal process does its work. Various
images flash through my mind, feelings swirl through me, and an
unconscious understanding of something I cannot put into words
begins to emerge. My therapist told me this might happen, but I am
not ready for how deep the changes go, the strength of the emotions,
and their diversity. I feel bombarded from everywhere inside as my

81

eyes follow the pencil; but as I relax in between, and focus on how I feel, something entirely unforeseen occurs. Slowly, I become aware of a deepening sense of resolution and peace inside brought about by the process. By the end of the session, the iron claw of my anger has loosened its grip.

§ § §

Between therapy sessions, the process continues to work on my brain and my body. In some moments, a deep understanding will suddenly well up, and in other moments, I can become extremely disoriented, seemingly out of nowhere. I begin to realize how central anger has been to my sense of self. Now that its hold is loosening, I am in an altered state. I begin to understand that my father passed his anger down to me, and that I have used the power of anger to fight against circumstances and people—and that then, in another self-twisting move, I rebel against anger itself and create a peaceful persona. Much of who I am has been formed as a reaction to anger, conscious or unconscious. Now I am disoriented without anger as the rudder with which to steer my life. I feel adrift, but I have found a new compass in meditation.

Daily meditation practice has my creative energy flowing, but my full-time job is boring and I feel frustrated. At work I feel lethargic, trapped, unfulfilled. Christmas is around the corner, and the dreadful depression of going through the holiday season without my family is lurking in the background of my mind. I feel lonely for the affection and joy we once shared together. It has been a long four years since I've seen my family on Christmas Day. I call my ex-wife and ask if I can come by this year to be with our kids. After checking it with the boys, she says, "Okay." I look forward to seeing them with all my heart and soul.

§ § §

On Christmas when I show up a little after noon, they are about to sit down to an early holiday dinner. I am astonished when they don't invite me to the table, and I have to elbow my way in to share the prayer with them. They eat while I watch and listen. When they raise their glasses in a toast, I am not included. Maybe it's the awkwardness of the situation, but it seems to me that my family is ignoring me; I feel as if I am being treated with less respect than a stranger would get. In the past, a situation like this would have made me extremely angry. This time I stay calm, but feel very, very sad.

A few hours later, as I drive home, I am blindsided by strong emotions that well up. I can't drive. I pull the car over to the side of the road and cry. Once home, a second flash flood of tears comes. The hot, dry desert inside me that always stayed parched by my constant flaring anger is now muddy and wet. My heart is no longer kept from feeling and, in this case, weeping. The tears feel good coming out; they are rinsing the residue of anger from my newly awakened heart.

§ § §

As I settle into this experience of being more in touch with the sad, quiet part of me over the next several weeks, my inner emotional terrain begins to change. This new view of the world, and my dawning understanding as to the source of my anger, is helping to sort my head and heart out. I see for the first time that I actually cause my own anger. This is tremendously freeing to know—not just to think, but also to truly see and feel and understand. No one is "at fault" when it comes to my anger. That twisted up notion came from an identity pattern I no longer find useful. Only I can take responsibility for my choice to use anger's power. The most liberating recognition of this comes when I am in a restaurant one day. For the first time I know I actually have a choice, and I pull the plug on a tirade before it happens. My girlfriend is confronting me with an accusation that I am withdrawing my affection and I feel the urge to escalate into anger. I can feel the polarization happen and I sense her anger grow too. And then, a bolt of lightening strikes at my old way of thinking—there are other choices! This is the first time I remember thinking this during a moment when my anger is beginning to rage. I am able to respond to the thought, and, in this moment, consider my options, and behave in a different way. I feel much better for it.

§ § §

Years later, as I am marching down the San Francisco streets protesting the bombing of Iraq, I am hit with a similar planet-

quaking notion as I feel anger about the giant superpowers, which push whole cultures and nations around with such powerful forcing currents. Everything around this behavior tends to generate more anger. But our peaceful protest reactions are alternatives to angry burning or killing. We are being a public example of another choice besides bombing, a choice of seeking an end to bombing—a choice being embraced by millions of people worldwide today.

We live in a world where anger is rampant, a powerful force that daily grabs humans by the throat and drags them to death's door in the name of God and revenge. Anger, except in the most blatant and unbalanced of its expressions, often is not even frowned upon. We excuse it in ourselves and in each other far too easily, particularly if our wish is to live in a friendly, peaceful world.

But to move out of anger's self-righteous, blaming stance and into a place of more openhearted tolerance and acceptance requires tremendous courage. Anger is really a cowardly way out of a collision with someone. It's a sure-fire way to shut the heart down and narrow the range of another person's options. To stay in the moment and locate the root of anger in one's own body-mind, as it unfolds, requires fierce willingness and vigilance. Once located, the root can be yanked out—gently and with a firm grip of love and understanding—but it requires the greatest courage of all. More courage than I had the first time I made the passage. What makes anger so hard to let go of is that it leaves you empty for a moment, empty and naked. Oddly enough, however, there is a quiet strength that can fill that void and clothe you with a royal robe of grace. When you feel it, you know what made people like Gandhi and Martin Luther King great. *The power of peace far surpasses the blowtorch of rage.* It is a cool, pervading, persisting power that eventually penetrates illusion and sets the heart free. This is true power, and it is inside each one of us. The authentic power of peace is the opposite of rage, it is the brilliant aikido sleight-of-hand that liberates rather than strikes.

To know this is to grow more mature in a profound and irreversible way. The beauty of the current state of evolution is that humanity is in the process of outgrowing its adolescent rages, and maturing towards peace on a collective level. Our generation of Boomers and the Peace Movement are the ones that started making this evolving sense of peace visible. The false power of domination and tyranny are past their heyday and are now on the decline. The authentic power of peace and respect for diversity is here to stay. *I firmly believe that as far as evolution is concerned, failure to achieve peace on Earth is not an option.*

Tyranny's reign has left humankind scarred with anger. At the roots of my anger I find the most powerful negative force currently being expressed in our world. This power is within each and every one of us, and is rampant in our systems. All trails of abuse and violence lead to the feet of this particular power of tyranny. Using this power, unconscious attitudes many of us chose in youth run us like invisible programs fed into a computer. This power involves the mind and will, combined with the forcing current in a hideous manner. Anger is created and fuelled by this power. I call it "the Judge."

What does it take to judge? What cognitive process do you use to make your judgments? What are the forces of energy involved in judging? Blaming, shaming, and punishing are intentions most of us harbor when we judge. The judge takes its job of being a demi-god quite seriously and strives to assert its will, or at least its opinions, on others—imposing a certain set of standards, rules, laws, assumptions, expectations, and desires on people, as well as situations.

Let's look deeper at the function of this aspect of mind. And let's consider another, similar, but very different function: discernment. How does judgment differ from discernment? Discernment is more objective; it seeks to perceive reality clearly and in a functional way rather than in a context of taking things in a personal way. It is a clear perception and recognition of what is so. Judgment is far more subjective. Judgment compares what's so with a set of standards set by some group, or with personal standards we have set for ourselves. Judgment is an opinion that has a punishing element when forced on those whose opinion, belief, or standards we disdain.

When we judge others, we actually hurt *ourselves*. If we allow the mind to take a self-indulgent, righteous, indignant stance when others don't do what we want, then our stubborn ego is tyrannized and controlled by the judge. A short-term gain—the feeling of being "better than"—may bolster our sense of importance for a moment, or a season, yet nothing is ever accomplished but more judgment and anger.

As humanity moves upward on evolution's spiral, we now learn that *synergy*—cooperation, not righteousness—is what really leads us to progress. Cooperation starts with communication, consideration, and compassion; cooperation places a primary emphasis on the understanding shared between people. *Once we take into account the feelings and needs of those we share our world with, be they family or neighbors or nations, we naturally act in greater accord with what works for everyone involved.* Understanding others expands our mind and heart, making our attention more all-inclusive, our intention more noble, and our intelligence more focused on solutions than complaints. Part of the synergy of this is that to understand the feelings and needs of others, we must also understand our own.

Often rather than understanding our feelings we indulge them by imposing them. Imposing our feelings on others rather than communicating clearly is a way of saying, "I am the center of the Universe. It all spins around me. What I want is all that is important." No wonder people have so many relationship problems; when we act like we are the center of the universe—the only center—we keep bumping into one another's free will. This results in abuse and violence of all kinds. A long outmoded survival program, the judge kicks into gear; we see those who do not agree with what we want as "in the way." This approach is practically useless now on Earth. When we allow this program to persist, it continues to give the reins of human tyranny to the Judge.

It is a beautiful autumn day and I am borrowing some tools from a friend. Taking advantage of the excuse for a visit, we sit and talk: catching up with each other's life, joking about our situations, telling our dreams and visions. Afterwards, I am high from the wonderful discussion, floating in the warm glow of shared camaraderie and bonding, thankful for the inspiration and spiritual understanding I share with my friend. As I bask in a feeling of oneness with the universe, I bend down to load a cement cinder block in my car.

Suddenly, I spot a big black spider with a red hourglass marking. "Black widow!" My brain screams, the unity experience of a moment before vanishes, as I feel a rush of adrenaline impulse me to kill the spider before it kills me. I smash the spider with the cinder block.

Suddenly, I realize where the impulse toward exterior force comes from. The impulse to kill was an immediate response when my survival was threatened. With or without fear, eliminating the threat and stopping the spider from hurting anyone was the only solution. Everyone concurred, there was nothing else I could do.

Rarely do we face an immediate threat to our survival that announces itself as blatantly obvious as the black widow spider. Without clear and present danger that warrants decisive action, we become partially paralyzed, unable to muster the will and conviction required to deal with the obvious threats to the survival of our species. A feeling of powerlessness results from sensing this impending doom all around us, it exasperates us because we have no way to fight and no place to flee, so we take external force in hand and vent our frustration to dispel this sense of impotence. "If only everyone would listen to me, and do it my way!" With no visibly immediate threat to facedown or tackle, our mind, propelled by the forcing current, steps into the position of judge, jury, and executioner. We then dump our highly charged frustration and emotional energy on those around us in an attempt to control them, as if our agenda were a matter of life or death.

Under the influence of this unconscious force, we feel the intensity in our solar plexus, as adrenaline pumped nerves move us to fight or flight. This is when we use whatever ammunition is at hand: sex, money, power, ego-manipulation, etc. I cannot count the times I ruined a relationship with attitudes that said, "Forget the judge, and get me the executioner! I've had it!" I even used these same tactics on myself saying, "I haven't done anything useful with my life. I am nothing; I'd be better off dead."

This is the pattern I wrestled with after my divorce. I felt worthless, and deserving of the disdain I imagined my family felt toward me. I felt stupid and guilty; I had made a number of bad choices. I no longer trusted myself. I had to admit my behavior deserved to be punished, and I did not cut myself any slack when it came to punishing myself. I felt so sick of myself that my constant state was misery. This went on for three years. The judge inside me wouldn't quit, and kept beating me down at every turn. My internalized, unresolved anger erupted time and time again, surfacing in all my relationships. I would take every relationship to the same desolate place, playing and replaying the same old movie—with my rage being the biggest judge of all. After a while, like a phoenix, consumed in the flames of my anger, I eventually rose from the ashes with a new movie.

Ramana Maharshi said, "Life is a movie starring the ego, directed by Karma and produced by Maya."

The stories we tell about who we are and why things happen the way they do seem to run along predictable plot lines if we pay close attention. The victim in our favorite story is usually the hero too. In our story, the victim who is judged by others as worthy of abuse, neglect, or violence, is also the hero of our story trying to overcome overwhelming obstacles in life as a normal person. Our stories are so very convincing that we begin to believe the movie is real. *This is because something amazing happens as we talk to others and tell our story—we re-experience it!* When we do this, we believe we are our movie. We replay the same movie over and over, we even start talking to the characters, and then wonder why the characters don't change and why they keep answering or ignoring us the same way each time. Believing our movie is real, we forget to go home and live our lives, instead we stay in the theater and keep replaying the drama, hoping for a different ending that never comes.

The principle character writing our movie—the one who creates the victim, or the hero, or the oppressor—is the judge. The judge loves to stir up trouble. If you have ever tried to work or socialize in a room where the judge is active in somebody's attitude, you know what a showstopper that presence can be. We sense the judgment in a person's tone of voice, their words, gestures, and the lack of all these, too. We can feel judgment physically when it is directed our way, or when we exert judgment towards others, or when we imagine it. When we judge ourselves, we usually imagine judgments others would place on us—our parents, lovers, children, friends, neighbors, teachers, bosses, etc. Strangely enough, we then often try to get them to agree with our judgments upon ourselves, and if they do not agree with us, we punish them for not seeing our guilt. Judging them guilty for not agreeing with our judge, we treat them as if they are as guilty as we think we are. Needless to say, this causes most of the confusion we emotionally experience when we are hit from all the angles and positions held by the judge. Our body feels these crosscurrents as nervous energies with conflicting signals of fight or flight.

Now we are starting to see how insidiously the judge exerts its false power. At its own convenience, it puffs itself up, becoming whatever type of judge it wants to be at the time: the mild-mannered epicure, or the roaring accuser; the public assailant or private naysayer; the community cop or intimate finger-pointer; the patronizing know-it-all or arrogant pretender. The color of the judge's robe may change, but the judge is still the judge, and his gavel strike is always sharp and hard.

As I began to become more conscious of this, I realized that the judge works against me no matter what. Over time, I came to see that with any judge in the room, meaningful conversation became relatively impossible. Whether the judge was presiding in me or in others, as soon as one judge picked up his gavel, the judge in everyone else would show up in one way or another. Sparks would start to fly between us, everyone's gut would tie a knot, and all real listening would come to a stop. When the judge holds court, the only communication allowed is defense or prosecution. Tolerance goes right out the window.

In contrast, I remember many moments with a person or a group when I felt oneness, peace, and affectionate bonding. At those times, the judge was off duty. Tolerance held the space with an attentive presence, which made an ease of communication and sharing possible. Have you ever noticed how fast the tension is increased when the judge is present? Can you feel the judge when it is present in you? The judge is present before any accuser, jury, or punisher gets into action; they all wait for the judge to get their cue. Strangely enough, if the judge never shows up, neither does the rest of the judiciary crew.

Sooner or later, the judge finds an accuser presenting a case before him, rehearsing as if reviewing a court brief for an upcoming trial. Then together, they spring the trial, picking jurors who share their values. One of my pet peeves on this is when a girlfriend of mine drags out into public an accusation that calls for a judgment from others about my behavior. When we are on trial, we often respond by putting the judgmental aspect of our accuser on trial. This can escalate into seceding from the union, which creates war in the case of nations and creates hell in the case of personal relationships.

Intimate relationships are torture when the judge's court is where couples relate to one another. Our mates can be our harshest judge, or our most candid mirror; either way it is a razor's edge we walk when we have to live with critical reflection in our face everyday. Tremendous power is unleashed in relationships when we drop the judge. Judgment can lead to grudges that destroy relationships. Even in the best relationships people find themselves constantly tempted to judge. In intimate relationships where love is deeply present, we find the motivation to compromise our ego. This ego death is the power of the spiritual marriage path, which leads to union with God. Through the heart's natural affection, we find the strength to silence the judge, and accept the other for who they are, complete with human limitations and divine perfections. *This is the beginning of true unity with another: accepting and embracing their total being.*

The best foundation for any relationship is laid by learning to do this within our self first. Breaking co-dependency, we land in an autonomous realm where we are free to accept and appreciate another. We become self-responsible, and own up to our experience rather than judge and blame others for it. If we start from self-acceptance, with a healthy self-image and without angry judgment, our relationships can enter into true partnerships. Our energy is enabled in a completely new way when we ally our powers. Co-creation and harmony become available. Living becomes artful. Most of us are not taught this harmonious style of co-creative artfulness in school, nor in most family traditions of behavior. Each of us discovers and learns it as part of the lessons of our life. In our own way we find how to dance with life. We each find a functional way that works for our personal growth, a way that changes the old patterns we are stuck in, a way that liberates us from the judge.

Transforming the old ways and learning to stop the judge before he takes over, requires learning the secret of where the judge comes from. This secret is so simple it needs no hiding. *The secret is in a shift of perception. Instead of perceiving through the eyes of the judge, we look through the eyes of our authentic power.*

That shift enables us to see what is right in front of us all the time: right now is always the choice point as to whether we will call the judge up. This is because it is also always right now that we must decide how to deal with the frustration of not getting what we want or getting what we don't want. In this moment we humans are blasted with experiences so diverse and multilayered, influencing us to judge whether we can accept our experience or try to change it, that we ignore most of them and only deal with the familiar ones. *But in reality, the only choice is to accept the experience or reject it.* Rejecting it takes the judge, accepting it takes discernment.

Discernment is the ability to determine in an instant whether or not we are in a "do-or-die" situation. Judgment makes us act like we are faced with a choice between life and death. Without discernment, the judge comes forward with all of his power. Discernment is the sword that helps us cut through the stranglehold of judgment. It is more objective, clearer, and has a broader range of perception. Discernment is also a spotlight that allows us to turn our attention on our attitude toward getting our needs and wants satisfied. What is real about our needs? Are they needs or wants? Do we know what we want? Can we define it? What happens inside when we get what we want? What happens inside when we don't get what we want?

As we do this type of self-examination, it becomes obvious that we don't always get what we want. Our attitude in the face of that stark reality becomes important. What thought processes and emotions kick into gear when we don't get what we want? Do we question the emotions that lead to the same old ineffective patterns when we don't get what we want? Questions like: "Is this a matter of life or death? Do I really need this, or am I responding out of fear, lust, insecurity, pride or ego?"

Here is the real work: to take in hand these tools, as we are learning them, and to find the authentic inner power, which understands that external power, forcing current, anger, fear, and judgment can be dropped. We *can* find ways to stop the judge in us, and cease punishing others and ourselves. To do this takes knowing we are worthy of divine love, worthy of our own love, and worthy of others' love. It takes knowing we are not our personal story, but rather a part of the process of evolution that is wrestling in all humans right now. Most importantly, it takes opening our heart and loving our self first. To love our self we must also learn to love others, for it is then that we are shown the parts of our self that others see and we don't. So how do we do that? Let's look at what doesn't work any more, and then look at what is working more than ever before.

You are aware of many of the things we have been talking about. For a number of generations now, the collective mind has been noticing what doesn't work any more—anger, external power, judging, abuse, and violence. Let's ask ourselves a few questions here. What does not work anymore both in our world and in our relationships? The expression "As above, so below" encourages us to look at our personal lives *and* also see what is similar in the world's circumstances.

For the sake of environmental and ecological survival, we could say that pollution by carbon emissions caused by burning oil, coal, and wood is one thing that really doesn't work anymore. The destruction of the rainforest the defoliation of the Earth doesn't work anymore. Who really owns the petroleum of the Earth? What historic civilization has the actual rights to it—if any? Is it true that some sheikh can make a billion dollars a day from it? Is it fair to burn as much as we do in the US if it is all so limited a resource and non-renewable?

Then there is the idea that democracy is not a consensus but a majority rule. The minority interests therefore are never represented in government. For government to represent the true interests of the people takes recognizing that when dealing with populations like 260 million people, 2.6 million people are only one percent. Every time one percent of the population is not in agreement with something imposed on them by a majority, they will drag their feet. This means every time one percent drags, the energy of 2.6 million people drains our country's collective efforts.

For instance, the presidential election of 2000 was contested and called illegal by many. That drags a lot of energy, and yet the man sworn in as president was placed in a position where he could use his power and declare war. As a result, the opposition to his policies hit the streets by the hundreds of thousands. Worldwide, in major cities, opposition added up to millions of people demonstrating against the war.

And when it comes to the Judge, can you see how it relates to relationship? Do you see how the judge is the cause of human suffering on the Earth right now? Can you recognize the judge inside of you as similar to the one outside? Do you try to enlighten the judge?

For instance, the US government declared the world's number one natural resource—hemp—illegal, in 1937. Since then, deforestation, oil pollution, and pharmaceutical industries have inflicted an unhealthy environment upon all of the people of the world. This illegal resource is so powerful that if you combine together all 3.5 million types of plants on the Earth you cannot equal what hemp can provide for fiber, fuel and medicine. It is the most prolific worldwide source of a renewable natural resource that exists.[8]

Instead of accepting this fact, the US judge decides to incarcerate over 200,000 citizens a year for the last twenty-five years. In 2002, a total of 750,000 people were arrested for possession of pot, with an estimated 12 million daily smokers breaking the law. Because of our moral judgment about people getting high, we have outlawed all other uses for this plant, such as fiber for clothing (without the polluting pesticides necessary for cotton), pulp for paper (no more trees cut for newspapers), seeds for oil and plastic and medicine (the greatest reducer of cholesterol in the natural world), bio-mass for fuels (hemp out-produces every other plant for this), and a replacement for wood. Instead of exploiting this prolific, renewable resource for our human needs, the US insists on making the oil industry richer. The facts have been proven scientifically: hemp can replace all petroleum uses, anything made of wood can be made of hemp, even cracking the hemp seed oil molecule can make plastic, and meshing its fiber and pulp together creates a light-weight building material that has the tensile strength of steel.[9]

But the judge inside the politicians' hearts calls it a drug, an evil "gateway" drug. Even in spite of medical proof that it is a medicine, even with citizens' initiatives passing laws to that effect in eight states, even still the US government uses military force against its citizens, illegally, to fight hemp. This one plant, which can do so much for our human needs right now on this polluted planet, is still seen by the government as an enemy.

Meanwhile, the government cocaine-heroin connection keeps making money for their illegal covert operations, and the greatest money-laundry in the world's history buys and sells armaments and drugs for their own profits to spend on their own secret agendas. The harm from these truly toxic drugs runs rampant. More than twice the numbers of people die of prescribed drugs than illegal drugs, while no one has ever died from a marijuana overdose.

But, that's enough of my own judgments for now. I could argue that this is discernment, but then one person's discernment might be another's judgment. My heaven could be your hell; your ceiling could be my floor.

The value inherent in the experience of life goes way beyond the mere instinct for survival; there is a quality of life that the human experience seeks. Sure we need to be able to take care of some very basic things first, like food, water, and shelter—but there is something yet unattained, yet unachieved, yet to be satisfied. We seek it as if it is the answer to our every problem—no matter how much we get what we want, most of us are not satisfied. We either want more or we want something else. *True satisfaction only comes when we master our attitude toward getting what we want or not getting what we want.* Disappointment goes along with dissatisfaction and frustration. Eventually we begin to realize that we need to be careful about what we want, because we might get it and not like it when we do. Often we find out after getting what we want that we really want something else. War is a tragic example.

When Americans went to war with each other in the 1860s, it was a time of murderous ruin. More Americans died in that war than in all the other US wars combined from then until Vietnam—including World Wars I and II. The devastation went deep into the South and North, leaving raped widows and orphans in its wake. The pre-war fervor was like an emotional competition, with old school rivals in sport. But the reality of the Civil War was so bloody and far-reaching that it left deep emotional scars. People realized that it was not a glorious war or a very intelligent war; in fact they deeply regretted having gone to war at all. The results were unavoidable: poverty, illiteracy, and ignorance. Hundreds of thousands were left bereft over the loss of loved ones, homes and lands. A whole swath of America was left to die in poverty, grief, and sickness.

Today, the emperor does not wear clothes at all—he stands naked in Iraq, claiming to wear a royal robe of democracy—one that proves to be invisible under close scrutiny. His motives are transparent, despite media coverage that tailors information around the naked truth. The real story is implied by what is not said; accurate information must be read between the lines or found through reliable sources on the Internet because "official" information uses lies disguised as truth. The world watches as the emperor's nudity is exposed, and the military industrial tailors standing by his side are likewise defrocked.

Discernment and common sense can keep the judge from interfering in our lives. They can also tell us when it is time to speak up and point out what we are discerning and what we see as common sense. *Staying silent allows only the loud bullies to be heard.*

Put the judge aside for a moment. Doesn't it feel wonderful? Imagine there are no valid judgments possible against anyone, and no valid excuses for war because we can use other resources to achieve unity. Imagine we use compassion and actually listen to someone like a homeless person; really hear him or her, and share in the human experience of his or her life. Imagine we listen to the story of an incarcerated person, or the stories of families who have loved ones who are sick and dying and have no money. Imagine we can listen to the famine-starved women who have nothing for their children to eat. Imagine we hear the voices of all who have been steamrolled by the modern age, the indigenous peoples, the endangered species, and the wilderness forms of life; imagine we hear and listen to them all with compassion.

CHAPTER SIX

Imagine just for a moment that you have the choice to create a world—a world that does not need war, because all people are treated with respect and compassion. Imagine you and millions of others like you doing this altogether. Feel in your heart the connection with all who ever prayed for or envisioned this. Then turn your eyes to the future of futures, and see a world where humans attain their fullness, when the memories of external power are but fairy tale lessons read to children that they might learn how to deal with the bestial ancestry of our bodies, and aim at the holy grail crown of creation called "Human."

7

BETWEEN DA FENCE, DA WALL, AND DA NILE

Imagine there's no countries, it isn't hard to do,
Nothing to kill or die for, no religion too,
Imagine all the people living life in peace…
—JOHN LENNON

In meditation, I imagine I am a young boy in Iraq when the tyrant's iron fist knocks down my walls. I stand naked, powerless, and alone. Exposed and vulnerable, I experience tyranny directly and know what a victim of terrorism feels. I watch helplessly as my family dies torturous, painful, deaths. I am told what to think, and given a choice to agree or die. I am put to work as a slave, until my body has no use and is discarded. I am forced to murder or be murdered. I am told how to live. My death occurs in a manner of someone else's choosing. There is no hope. I am aware in the meditation that this is the sort of tyranny the Middle East has suffered for centuries; it is also the legacy of power's abusive reign throughout time.

I remember feeling horrified as a child when I learned that such tyranny occurred in our world. Back then it was the Russian roulette form of tyranny: people of Berlin were shot in the back when they tried to cross the Iron Curtain, seeking freedom from the tyrants of Communism.

The Berlin Wall came down in 1990. The symbol of separation between Communism and Democracy, the wall was a source of contention because of the tyranny it enforced on those who were killed while trying to escape. Recalling the tyranny I have witnessed in my life, it seems obvious that *they all involved some sort of power used in a threatening and controlling manner—with weapons used to enforce their way.* The bullyboys need weapons. They need to carry them all the time because people might just resist their "law and order," and try to escape over their walls. The bullyboys force people to stay on the right side of the wall. The only way they can get away with it is through the use of weapons. Without weapons no one would listen to a bully or put up with them for long. Actually, the use of weapons builds walls. We defend and attack from our well-fortified walls with weapons we aim at the walls of others.

An epic rock opera for our time, *The Wall*, by Pink Floyd explores a personal and intimate perspective on the roots of tyranny within each individual. Performed live in concert during the 1980s and later released as a movie, *The Wall* can be seen as a modern allegorical drama about that which lives inside each of us, that which perpetuates war. Illustrating with music, lyrics, and visuals, *The Wall* uses war as a metaphor for personal growth.

The most troublesome and elusive tyrant of all lurks inside each of us. Beneath our mask of civilized normalcy, all of us hide the real perpetrator of war. *The wall we build inside that justifies war is based on denial.* "Da Nile ain't just a river in Egypt," goes the old saying; but when it comes to defending the wall, denial is tyranny's handmaiden. Tyranny and terrorism are two sides of the same coin, which is to say they are two different expressions of the same impulse—the urge to impose our will on others.

Pink Floyd performed *The Wall* live in concert only a few times during the spring and summer of 1980, shortly after the album zoomed up the charts to Number One and stayed there for five weeks—unprecedented for a double album. Roger Waters wrote the dramatic screenplay, and in 1982 *The Wall* was released as a full feature film directed by Alan Parker and starring Sir Bob Geldolf in the title role. Although an epic that is fantastic and incomparable on stage, *The Wall* on screen filled in many important and obscure details difficult to render in a live performance. The story makes real the grave cost of war, reveals the folly of denying human feelings, and boldly challenges the viewer to examine his or her own walls.

The Wall is more than a metaphor; as a constraint and ruling force within consciousness, it is all too real. It can be seen in the countless belief structures and attitudes that separate us from each other. In its harshest expression, it manifests as war. When we wall ourselves off, disregard our fellow human beings and fail to sense and see that they, too, have human needs and feelings, we set the stage for war. Although this has been so for millennia, the fact that it persists when we have at our fingertips the means to destroy all life on Earth is unprecedented. It is precisely this predicament that is pushing us up the ladder to our next step in evolution. In order to survive our own advances, we must develop a new form of intelligence, one that enables us to communicate effectively, move beyond our own limited attitudes, and so survive the threat to our species that is of our own making. This is the lethal paradox we are living.

Each time I watch *The Wall*, I see more deeply into the architecture of its mythos. As an entertainment choice, it is definitely not for Pollyanna types who prefer to be distracted or amused rather than challenged to think. Roger Waters, who wrote not only the concept and screenplay but the music and lyrics for *The Wall*, describes it this way: "...it's partly about not letting people go off and be killed in wars, but it's also partly about not allowing rock and roll, or making cars, or selling soap, or getting involved in biological research, or anything that anybody might do...not letting that become such an important and jolly boys' game that it becomes more important than friends, wives, children, or other people."[10]

Throughout *The Wall*, this theme runs parallel with the deep human need to share feelings. In the 1990 live Berlin show, produced by Waters with an international all-star cast, we see Pink, the main character in the script, wall up his feelings brick by brick by brick. We see that, when taken to an extreme, the inability to communicate feelings leads to a numbness so chilling that humans turn into tyrants. Without any capacity to feel or care for the feelings of others, the tyrant imposes his will and values on others. Repressing his own vulnerability, the bully beats down all opposition, and creates fear among those he exploits.

In the movie, Pink is on a concert tour far away from home. Feeling lonely, he calls his girlfriend, but the phone just rings and rings each time he dials. We see his girlfriend running around with an activist friend, having a great time in her lover's absence. When Pink finally gets through on her telephone line, a man answers and then hangs up. Pink spins out of control. In confused and jealous agony, he ritually prepares himself to overdose and commit suicide.

Glimpses of Pink's childhood are seen throughout the movie. His father, a British soldier, was killed in World War II and his widowed mother had to raise him alone. His only male role models were war heroes in the movies, cowboys like the Lone Ranger and John Wayne on television, and the bully schoolteachers who berated him at every turn. We watch as the young man constructs a thick wall around his hurt feelings. We see the dysfunctional communication patterns develop as Pink's emotional world shrinks and he becomes less and less capable of putting words to his feelings. His guitar and playing music are his only avenues of expression as he wails through the wall between his heart and the audience, pleading, "...is there anybody out there?"

Despondent at having been rejected, and feeling alone and alienated from the world, Pink commits suicide. But he is not allowed to die. His manager, whose only concern is money and contracts, finds a doctor to pull Pink back from the precipice of death. "The show must go on!" asserts his manager, with no concern at all for the feelings that pushed Pink to the edge. When Pink is injected with a drug that brings him back, we see him go through a psychedelic passage in which he is simultaneously transformed and possessed. He is dragged into a limousine and rushed to the show. When he finally arrives on stage, he has become a uniformed Nazi tyrant.

Turning against his audience, Pink orders his most loyal fans to "separate the riff raff...up against the wall!" In the next scenes, we see the streets overrun by his loyal fans who are rioting, burning, looting, and raping while the music plays "You better run." Next, we see Pink rip off his dictator uniform and begin to scream, "I'm crazy!" and break into an introspective song. A dreamy chorus, singing, "He's crazy," answers him. Next we see Pink, despondent, sitting on the floor of a public toilet cubicle in the concert hall, wondering if he's really been guilty of not deserving love all these years. He wails at the isolating wall inside of him, "There must have been a door here when I came in!" as we see a security guard approach the toilet stall.

In answer, the mighty worm judge appears, and a trial starts with the prosecutor charging Pink with the crime "...of showing feelings of an almost human nature." His mother, his schoolteacher, and his wife are all called to testify against him. Listening to their testimony, the judge becomes so enraged at Pink, he declares the trial over with no need for a jury: "Since my friend, you have revealed your deepest fear, I sentence you to be exposed before your peers. Tear down the wall!"

The walls tumble down dramatically, leaving nothing but rubble in the streets. Little children are picking up bricks where they find them, and the movie ends with the slightly hopeful lyrics,

> ...All alone, or in twos,
> The ones who really love you
> Walk up and down outside the wall.
> Some hand in hand.
> Some gathering together in bands.
> The bleeding hearts and the artists
> Make their stand.
> And when they've given you their all,
> Some stagger and fall; after all it's not easy
> Banging your heart against some mad bugger's wall.

This rock-opera classic artistically connects the dots between blocked and repressed human emotion and the travesty of war. The walls we build that pre-empt communication and healing are devastating to the heart, paralyzing and deadening to our feelings. Once the heart is numb, we find ourselves at war. Taking up arms and waging war could be called humanity's collective bad habit. Like all habitual behaviors, it is deeply entrenched. The idea that war issues forth from blocked communication about feelings may be more hindsight explanation than solution. But if we are intent on finding an alternative to war, the explanation is a useful pointer that can show us where to look for solutions. Whether we start by speaking our own repressed feelings or listening to those of others, realizing the devastating effect of building walls around emotion is a crucial, giant step to ending our habitual reliance on war as the solution to human problems. It all comes down to this: feelings we don't like get blocked, and we don't communicate our so very human vulnerabilities.

Outside the private realm of self-help, psychology, and spiritual development, feelings are rarely discussed. Human emotion is not addressed at all in our democratic process, and the feelings of the minority are not represented in government by their votes. The minority literally "loses." Americans have a strangely myopic view of reality: despite the fact that we comprise only seven percent of the world's population, our feelings, our needs, our lifestyle, (those of our elected majority) are the only ones that seem to count. Americans, on the whole, have constructed a massive wall of denial. We could call it "the Prosperity Curtain." Thrown up long before *The Ugly American* was published, it's what makes our fat cat, shit-don't-stink lifestyle outright disgusting. Forget the fact that people in third world countries envy us, that envy is as blinding as any curtain or wall. The Prosperity Curtain allows Americans to sit a comfortable distance from reality, while our small population exploits seventy percent of the world's natural resources. We devastate the environment in the service of an opulent lifestyle while leaving the rest of the world to live in poverty downwind from our stench.

Whether the tyrannical acts of the US government comprise war crimes or not will be up to a world court to decide. Meanwhile, Americans still like to believe in the notion that ours is a champion crusade to democratize the world. We are surprised when terrorists attack us. Forced to see the vast conundrum of denial and deception, we must come to grips with the fact that terrorism is largely a US government creation. Our government has funded, armed, trained, and employed terrorists worldwide for over forty years.

How would Americans feel if mom and pop's farm was taken, and they were forced to work at slave wages? What if we were given no viable choice other than to ship all the work and resources out of the country to wasteful, greedy gluttons overseas who only want more, more, more? What if we were forced to do business with people who funded despotic authoritarian regimes that deny our human rights? Americans stubbornly refuse to look at the truth about our government's involvement in violations of human rights all around the globe. Is the wall so high now that we can't see or hear any feelings? Does it hurt too much to think about it? Do you find yourself wishing you could stay comfortably numb?

The United States Constitution gives the people the right to rule themselves, but that right has been deeply undermined. Military-industrial complex control of the media, and secret boardroom allegiances between corporations and government, prevent the truth from reaching the American people. During the Vietnam War, the media showed us everything that was happening. We saw G.I. Joe getting killed—and murdering the Vietnamese—every night on the television. Real blood, real people, brought to us live—without a wall of censorship thrown up by corporate media. Our feelings woke up. We, as a people—not just a nation, but a people worldwide—rose up and stopped that war. We even pardoned the deserters and erased their crimes of treason for refusing to go to war.

Today, the media has a wall up so high Americans aren't allowed to see the coffins of fallen soldiers. We are precluded from having an authentic feeling reaction by a smoke screen of "double-speak" language. Humans defending their homeland are called "insurgents" and we are supposed to ignore any feelings about Iraqi kids having American bombs scar their memories with bloodshed and family ruin. We are discouraged from thinking about the actual human cost of war. Were we to contemplate the real pain our choices inflict on others, to feel it authentically, the flood of tears would wash out the wall of our denial.

As a whole, Americans stay busy behind their Prosperity Wall and cannot be bothered by uncomfortable feelings. We just want to get to work on time, have a double latte, and continue with business as usual. When a peace demonstration stops traffic, we bitch and moan into the cell phone. We pay our taxes and thus we are complicit in our contribution to the billions of dollars that fund an ongoing state of war. Our citizenry pays thirty-five percent or more of their income to the government in taxes; reinforcing a wall they don't want folks peering over. The military industrial complex gets its funds from that thirty-five percent.

At this point in history, thirty-five percent or more of our collective energy is spent on protecting our feelings with a "comfortably numb" buffer, which we create through our lifestyle as a society that gets rich from war. Most Americans do not really consider the effects of this war on others. Our only worry is that we might die in a terrorist attack; we do not care about anything else. Even dead and wounded children escape our consideration. Americans seem to be saying, "We don't care what it costs, destroy Iraq and kill them all if that's what it takes." There is not much public display in America of feeling the pain of others, like feeling the pain of the crying children of Iraq, who wail in the streets and the bombed out ruins of their wounded and dead families. America's wall keeps us comfortably numb from the reality of our country's foreign policies.

In 1990, within months of the Berlin Wall coming down, Roger Waters staged a live production of *The Wall* before 350,000 people with state-of-the-art, multi-media technology and an all-star, international cast. The event was broadcast via satellite to over 100 million homes. The stage was constructed so that Pink's huge wall was built on the exact site where the Iron Curtain had been. The epic proportions of *The Wall* and its theme were presented with a full orchestra and choral group accompanying world famous virtuoso rock musicians. The Russian Marching Band joined the cast on stage to play "Bring The Boys Back Home." High above the finished wall constructed on stage during the performance, two electric lead guitars wailed, giving hope that music would continue to pass the message over the wall. For the one-time-only production, Roger Waters wrote a special song to end the show. The complete ensemble of all-star performers sang that song for an ending that spread a tremendous message of hope. Reaching beyond what had been originally scored for the movie, the lyrics spoke of a future in which humanity might wrestle technology's power from the hands of the warlords, as "the tide is turning."

At this moment in history, humanity faces the possibility of mass extinction, brought about by our own hand. Destruction of all that is noble and beautiful in our world is imminent. We are on the verge of massive global suicide that could obliterate all other life forms on Earth. Our collective survival strategy of operating as if each nation state is separate and autonomous, sovereign in its own right without regard to the sovereignty of other nations, has resulted in an international Pandora's box of national and political walls.

The battle for territorial rights and natural resources, including human labor, has dragged us through millennia of war. In the last century, we developed the means to erase whole populations by dropping bombs from the sky; we now have the ability to kill entire populations without looking so much as one person in the eye. That is an unprecedented reality that has our collective consciousness and evolving conscience now raising a crucial question: "What authority gives any collective force the right to threaten, plan, tool up for, or actually use weapons of mass destruction?" If what we call "authority" is authentic and responsible, the question is easy to answer. But civilization as we know it has not evolved a means of governance that is authoritative in the authentic power sense. Not a single government or political body exists that has taken up a global integrity that would transform our world. The United Nations is an early attempt to accomplish just that, but UN authority has not been able to challenge the tyrannical forces whose military might and nuclear prerogative still play Russian roulette with the future of the human race and the future of our world.

Those who are forcing this predicament on humanity make vast sums of money from death and war. They make billions of dollars exploiting the last non-renewable natural resources of the Earth and going to war to maintain control of oil. They demand the right to decide what's best for other nations, and are willing to kill to make the point. Their authority is no more sophisticated than that of the biggest bully on the playground. Of real authority, they know nothing; vested interests obscure their ability to see the larger reality. Unrealistic demands are the result, and rational discussion is obscured. Information is censored and manipulated to support special interests. The facts are distorted and backed by bogus proofs. This was bad enough back in the days of Vietnam, but at least the media then had the freedom to broadcast the bloodiest footage, live, into our living rooms. That kept us in a state of shock about war.

Today, our government does not allow such freedom of information; they are intent on swaying public opinion about war. This is the government that allowed a Texas conglomerate to buy up eighty percent of all outside-of-the-home entertainment, including sixty percent of all adult prime time radio stations, ninety percent of all billboards, and eighty percent of stadiums, amphitheatres, coliseums, theaters, and concert halls. This is the company that banned "Imagine" by John Lennon and "Peace Train" by Cat Stevens during wartime, and has told even the biggest stars what songs they could and could not perform.

Under the guise of protecting our country from Internet hacker terrorists, the government also made public the fact that they have now developed software that can key in on certain words and grab e-mails. Pressure has been put on computer manufacturers to make this easy for them. Like Big Brother, the government breeds fear and paranoia, threatening publicly that they can track whoever visits controversial websites. Now anyone who uses a cell phone or e-mail can be tracked anytime, anywhere.

Obviously, the government's involvement in surveillance activities is based on a fear motive. And they have good reason to fear. After all, just .01% of the world population is about 650,000 people, and we have now seen that it takes far fewer dissatisfied humans than that to destroy a towering presence like the World Trade Center in New York City. In a world such as the one we live in today, majority rule makes little sense. With a population this huge, a whole new form of integrity in governing ourselves must come to the fore if humanity is to survive.

All people on this planet are locked together in our fate. Nuclear, biological, or any form of war, now threatens the survival of all humans. War today stimulates our deepest instinct: species preservation. Can you feel it? If you don't feel it, check out your walls and make sure they aren't really slaughterhouse ovens heating up.

The implications affect us deeply both on a personal level and as a collective. We must choose a new way to live or we will die.

Changing the world may be an impossible task for an individual to contemplate, but we can make a beginning by looking deeply into our personal wars, walls, defenses, and denials. What fears create our personal wars in life? What defenses protect our ego's pride? What realities and truths are we in denial of? What pains and abuses—"slings and arrows of outrageous Fortune"—cause us to react blindly and retaliate? What methods do we choose to achieve peace in our lives? Are we honest with others and ourselves? Are we telling lies, cheating, stealing, killing, and abusing—in emotional, mental, or sexual ways? Are we taking responsibility in our experience? Are we accountable for our behavior? Are we willing to take a risk and love our self and others? Are we bullying or tyrannizing others? Are we seeking to dominate or be dominated? *How can any of us really expect our leaders to have more integrity and learn the ways of peace if we don't do those things in our own lives?*

Take a look at the walls around your feelings. What emotions do you deny or block so much that a minor slight can cause you to explode with tyrannical force? Emotional bombs tick away inside many of us. Just watch what happens when people are safely sealed in a car and someone cuts them off on the freeway. Road rage is a telling but dangerous pressure release that speaks to the hotheaded effects of venting repressed feelings. Our own terrorist within reaches the point of desperate frustration, and says, "I can't take it anymore!" We bully our way through, or flip someone off in an explosive rage. Unfortunately, this does not always happen in the private safety of a car; repressed emotion can just as easily explode on members of our family and community.

One way or the other, feelings are always present. Even beneath extreme numbness are feelings that need to be heard. Staying numb doesn't work anymore, and we all have to figure this out, not just the isolated special-interest politicians. Everyone has the capability to be constructive and destructive. The choice, which is now pushed on humanity by evolution, is to become more constructive, especially about feelings. *We must use our feelings in a constructive manner to create systems that function on the basis of truth and accountability.* Disclosure of the facts as they relate to the health of the whole rather than private, vested interests that benefit the few while exploiting the many is imperative. Alternative systems are within our reach.

Perhaps the most hopeful and enlightened political document of the Twentieth Century was The United Nations' Declaration of Human Rights.[11] Almost every government on the Earth has signed this document since its inception after World War II. This document declares that every human being has the right to an environment that is free from fear. Also deemed as rights are a place to live, food to eat, health care, and education. This little-known document outlines a set of universally held human values that could be the standards of future governments.

The question becomes, how do we evolve government to represent all our human needs on Earth?

Our present political system doesn't work anymore. Fifty years ago, children were encouraged to imagine they could "grow up and be president someday." No one imagined it would cost hundreds of millions of dollars to run for president by the time we were old enough to try. Our elected representatives are supposed to represent the interests of their constituencies. But the more corrupt a system gets, the less politicians know of people like you and me whom they never meet. Their allegiance falls toward folks they see all the time when they get wined and dined. In a true consensus democracy, lobbyists are unnecessary.

Revolutions are unreliable and costly. Terrorism is a dead end. An Act of Congress to change the political process would have to be passed by the very people it would put out of office, and is therefore most unlikely. "What other recourse do we have besides being the bully on the block in today's world?" That is the question evolution prods Americans with now. How we act now to change is crucial to humanity's survival. If we look the other way, the government might continue to dominate every part of our lives, or it might evolve out of the way.

Remember the Aesop's Fable about the hungry wolf? The wolf comes out of his cave and raids the farmyard, grabbing as many animals as he can.

He throws them in a big bag, and runs back to his wolf den, only to be overpowered by all the critters when he opens the bag to devour them.

Imagine a world that doesn't need politicians or governments. Just for a minute, really imagine it. What if we had nothing to fear—no wars and no enemies? What if we could keep business as usual running with our collective energy? Taxes could become voluntary tithes to social, educational, health, and environmental developments of our individual choices (for example, I might give a percentage of my taxes to educational or environmental projects, while others choose to give to health and social services). If we relinquish our dependence on petroleum and develop alternative technologies; if we support the education, health, and welfare of all humans; if we disempowered all bullies by having no positions of power which could be abused (sure enough, if you create the power position, eventually someone will step in and abuse it; like Hitler, Stalin, or Saddam); but most of all, if we all learn to get along with each other and we consider our children's children for generations to come, we can actually live well and happy on the Earth.

The connection between the collective breakdown and personal malaise becomes obvious once we see that what doesn't work on one level doesn't work on any level. What hurts human society and politics also hurts our relationships. The politics of personal life that use avoidance, authoritarian laws, and enforcement all serve a special interest—self-centeredness. Keeping secret agendas and assuming authority enough to declare rationalized aggression ruins relationships between lovers and between nations. Then, whether we are talking about a divorce lawyer or a senate investigation committee, the expense of finding arbitrators to mediate our differences is more than just money, one that is not completely accountable and often relies on deception. *Wouldn't it be more expedient, and less costly all around, to forge our way ahead and find the way to establish a truly free, democratic relationship with our loved ones and the world?*

In so many ways, humans have devolved rather than evolved. We don't really talk to each other anymore, or rather; we don't listen to each other anymore. Control of information is as prevalent in the political realm as it is in our relationships. It's the same story in both arenas: sneaky, dishonest words that misrepresent our thoughts or intentions, clever words pursuing our own special interest agendas, spying on each other, suspecting dishonesty and harmful intentions, gathering circumstantial information about each other and using it to assert power and control.

We exploit the resources of other nations, much the same as we exploit energy in our relationships—in order to get what we want! We woo the third-world as if it were the farmer's daughter, we promise lots of goodies, but then we get out of town before having to explain or account for our behavior. Often in relationships we exploit the resources of another for our own profit, and then when the questions get asked that intimidate us with accountability, we leave the relationship rather than work it out. We build up our walls and get self-righteously defensive. We choose to go to war.

The choice to go to war is no longer intelligent! We must find more civilized, sophisticated, and enlightened methods to achieve our goals. War is an excuse for the emotional propagandists who would have us build their military industrial complex and make them rich. *In the noblest aspects of our humanity we recognize that the reverence for life makes war and murder obsolete. Revering life is a natural affection that comes from appreciating the experience of living. It is a sentiment most people share in common.* Humans are just folks. At least most are. Then there are the bullies, too scarred to remember how to be human rather than bestial. A bully picked one man as the target and over 1,000 American men and women are dead so far, a year and a half later. The murder was justified by lies and propaganda; the same type of empty rhetoric that we have heard come out of the mouths of government officials for centuries.

What people of other nations read between the lines about Americans from the imperialistic actions of our government hurts all of us. Our nation does not seem intelligent. For instance, why do we allow a position of power that is practically super-human in terms of armies, weapons, and armaments of destruction to continue to exist in the first place? What kind of person would have the true qualifications to fill that awesome position of power in this nuclear age—to be Commander in Chief of such a superpower as the United States? This is an important question, one that cannot be taken up seriously when military industrialists hold all the power.

Solar power lobbies and other new technologies are not yet able to compete with the lobbies of the petroleum, coal, and war industries. The only choice seems to be to dismantle all positions of power and not allow humans even near them. And certainly we would not feel comfortable with a non-emotional machine being in that power position either. But, to truthfully address the evolutionary energy of humanity right now is to accept that these power positions will not exist much longer, as they are archaic and more trouble than they are worth. Power will not be externally controlled anymore; it will be addressed authentically from within. From that place, the war is already over.

War will eventually be scorned for the atrocity it is and seen as the tool of murderers and bullies, unfit to be used by modern humanity. In the reality of our lives we do not allow immature children to play with dangerous and deadly objects, nor do we work for companies who decide to run off with our money and kill children with million dollar missiles. It is only common sense.

In fact, external wars will probably be banned in the near future, as more and more people appreciate the experience of all that life offers. From this perspective, the war walls can be seen as having sandbox foundations in reality; they are built upon the childish habits of bullies who claim, "Might is right." As the shifting sands of time flow into a new era, humanity faces fear, hatred, and survival from a different understanding—one that realizes war breeds fear and hatred, and leads us now to global suicide. With this understanding, we can leave our sandboxes and our sandcastle walls of war behind us. We can take on the truly challenging task of finding solutions that do not inflict violence on Life or in our lives. This is the foundation of lasting peace, much stronger and more enduring than any wall.

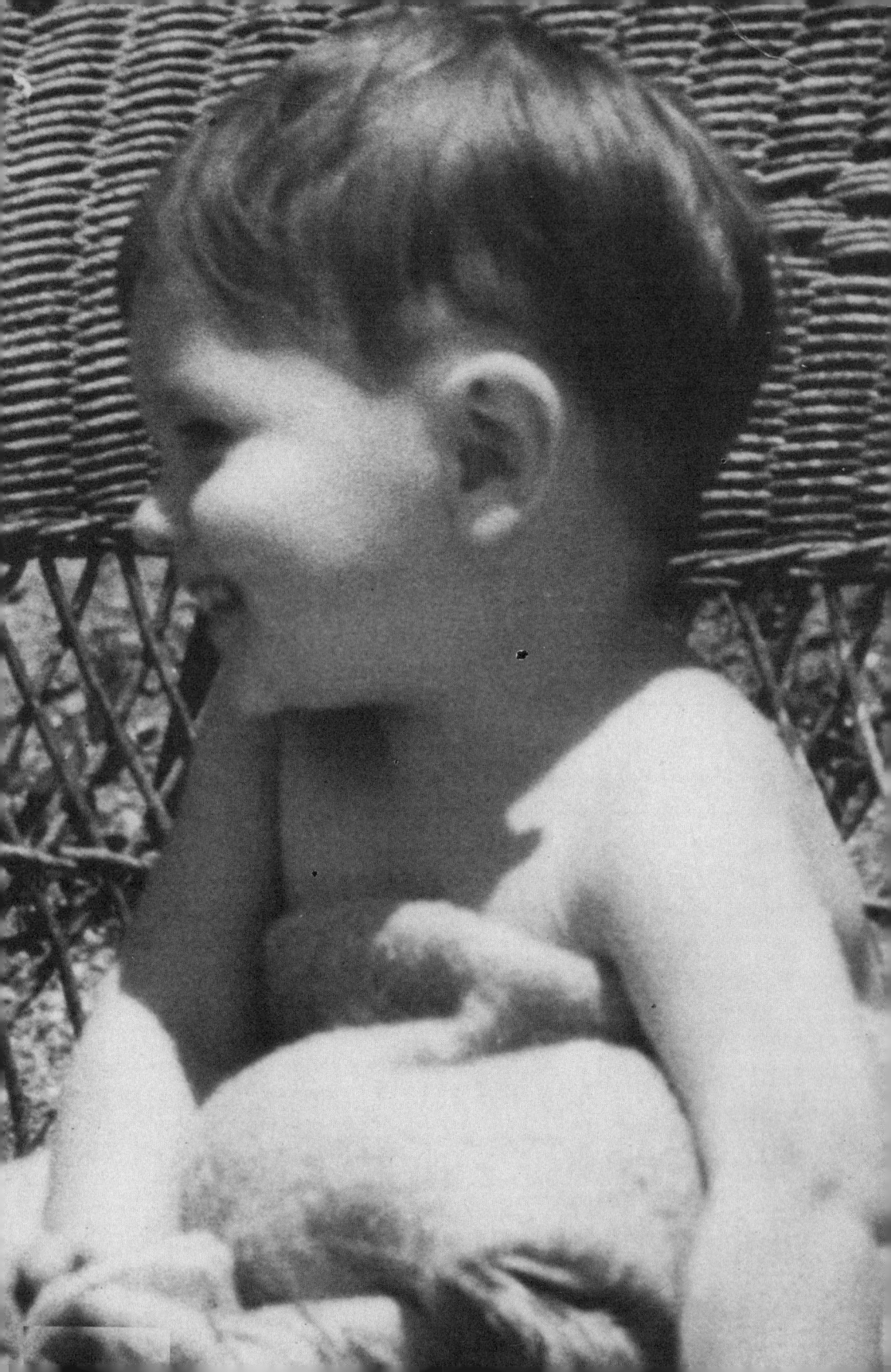

8

GROWING UP

I'll love you with all the madness in my soul
Someday girl I don't know when
We're gonna get to that place
Where we really want to go
And we'll walk in the sun
—BRUCE SPRINGSTEEN

In January 2002, leaders of all the major religions of the world convened in Assisi, Italy. Representatives numbering more than 200 came together just a few short months after the World Trade Center tragedy for an absolutely unprecedented historical meeting. Pope John Paul II and a number of cardinals were in attendance, as was Bartholomew I, spiritual leader of all Orthodox Christians, and twelve rabbis, some of them from Israel. Thirty Muslim imams from Iraq, Iran, Egypt, Pakistan, and Saudi Arabia, joined dozens of church ministers—Presbyterians, Baptists, Methodists, Lutherans, Anglicans, Disciples of Christ, Pentecostals, Mennonites, Quakers, Moravians, and the World Council of Churches. Hindus, Buddhists, Sikhs, Zoroastrians and native African religions sent their representatives.

Unanimously, these leaders proclaimed that, "Violence and terrorism are opposed to all true religious spirit and we condemn all recourse to violence and war in the name of God or religion." Furthermore, they declared, "No religious goal can possibly justify the use of violence by man against man... [using] religion to foment violence contradicts religion's deepest and truest inspiration." The result of that meeting was a document called the Assisi Decalogue for Peace[12] consisting of ten points that pledge to bring human rights, peace, and healing of the nations forward as a common priority among all religions.

Strangely, however, news of the Assisi Decalogue did not make headlines. The Enron hearings did, as did the seventeen people killed on the West Bank and the seven American soldiers killed in Afghanistan that same week. Leaders from all the world's major religions came together and denounced religious violence, but press coverage basically ignored the event, while unholy crusades and jihads made the headlines everyday.

The ancient questions of religion, philosophy, and morality become moot points at a time when the real burning question is, "Can humanity leap into a new awareness of our total interdependence here on planet Earth?" Forget the Emperor's new clothes, or which Emperor is in the White House. The house itself is on fire!

Humanity is only just beginning to recognize that we are part of a larger existence of life. The evolving universe has brought humanity into being after a billion trillion year thrust to finally manifest consciousness. The arrogant human ego claims the body as the self, when the body is the evolved result of all creation. This mighty human upstart, in merely a few more billion years, will be extinct, as evolution moves on.

Only blind ignorance or hideous arrogance can construct sufficient denial to negate our obvious connection to all life in this historic moment. Humanity is in possession of a remarkable alchemical ingredient in evolution: reflective consciousness, that refinement of intelligence that activates the potent force called *free will*. Reflective consciousness and free will are the same thing; they inherently exist together and can never be separated. Now humanity stares into the global mirror at itself, reflecting upon the wholeness no diversity can deny—the unity of Earth-bound bodies that rely on limited parameters for life. Our planet is our body; our physical bodies are composed completely of ingredients that come exclusively from the Earth.

Humanity is evolution waking up. We are 6.5 billion people, going downhill fast in a vehicle out of control, with no one in the driver's seat. At least, the collective consciousness of humanity has become more and more accessible as our library of information reaches around the globe. Soon, the obvious will be even more obvious: *unity is the result of specialized diversity.* Respecting and cultivating diversity integrates unity into a body of consciousness. The human mental ego is the many-headed beast seeking to devour and conquer anything it perceives as other than itself. *When this ego surrenders to unity and is tamed, the tyrant of the mind becomes the greatest servant.* It is even so clever it can accomplish tasks that call for a focus on unity and integration. For example, with "right mindfulness" and vigilance the mind can keep us in touch with our authentic power. Instead of reminding us of our past pains, it can remind us of our connection with the divine presence manifesting in this everlasting moment.

In 1994, mathematician John Forbes Nash (popularized in the movie "A Beautiful Mind") received the Nobel Prize in Economics for his "Game Theory," which he based on this premise: "All things in the universe work best when they work equally for their own good and for the good of all Creation." This truth, when focused on by the human mind, can reveal the optimal course.

Existence, consciousness, and bliss exist everywhere equally in all things. Only a veil of perception separates us from the bliss of our existence in this eternal moment: billions of molecules in rapturous harmony, every second creating and sustaining the existence of a human body. Bliss and consciousness exist as our true self—always present, always accessible— but ordinary awareness is blind to that condition of reality.

Extraordinary states are no longer completely foreign. An entire generation has gained access to these exceptional states through meditation, psychedelics, and disciplined spiritual practice. We have learned to relax, surrender, open, and allow the non-ordinary to emerge in our awareness. Our perceptual range has expanded.

Like the air and space everywhere we take for granted yet do not see, closer than this is the truth of self: existence, consciousness, and bliss. So close is the unified field, the mind must work extra hard not to perceive it. The mind must screen out a large percentage of incoming information to avoid being overwhelmed. Millions of synapses, hormones, nerves, and muscles respond to the exterior information with an overpowering program of individuality that protects the body, mind, emotions, and ego from getting lost in the cosmic soup of life.

I am three years old. With a start, I wake up to the sound of my mother and father screaming. My father is drunk and very angry. I see him slap my mother, and I see her wince in pain. I cry out in shock, hot tears flow down my face. My father turns and hits me, shouting, "Shut up and stop crying."

My shock becomes numbness and terror. I am disoriented and distressed. My body feels like an imprisoned volcano, my mind is so confused from the turbulent feelings that I inwardly retreat and long for my mother's arms to enfold me.

§ § §

Through the haze of the next several weeks, I am vaguely aware that my mother takes me and my younger brother on an airplane to Grandma's. My father is not around. My relatives are totally spoiling me and I feel less numb. The threat seems less immediate; my body is full of nervous energy. I start sucking my thumb all the time and wetting the bed at night, something I haven't done since potty training.

§ § §

A few months later, I am being given a lavish birthday party: friends come to play, and we have, cake, ice cream, and noisy party favors. We play pin the tail on the donkey, and I have more presents to open than I imagined could exist. I am the center of attention and this makes me very happy. My mother smiles and pats her growing womb.

A few days later, I notice some kind of commotion going on among the adults in the house. My mother, her folks, and her sister are having a heated discussion about things I cannot understand. Later, I learn that my father has been arrested during a burglary. His mother calls my mother and they talk for a very long time on the phone. My mother wants to believe that my father has had a total change of heart while in jail. She agrees to fly out and see him, hoping that it's true he is ready to mend his ways.

Seven months pregnant with twins, my mother goes into premature labor when the plane lands in Detroit. The twins have to be placed in incubators for over a month, and during that time, one of them dies. That is why my mother doesn't return right away as she had promised. But no one tells me what is happening. Grandma and Aunt Dorothy coddle me and constantly shower me with presents. A week goes by, and I begin to feel very strange. I sense that something important and dangerous is happening to my mother. All my infant mind can grasp is that my father has something to do with it.

Grandma gives me chocolate candy whenever she sees that I am sad and lonely for my mother. She makes me more and more batches of chocolate chip cookies. I learn to compensate for mother's missing love with chocolate and sweets. But no amount of chocolate can fill the hole left in her absence. I start making myself sick eating too much sugar. I can't shit. My feces get so hard and big they split my butt, I tear and bleed, and it hurts like hell.

Grandma is upset by this and forces me to take enemas. The long tube, yucky water, and totally icky feeling of the enema makes me even more upset. I resist Grandma, resist the toilet, refuse all food but sweets, and long more and more for my mother.

The feeling in my four-year-old body is a steady, growing ache. I deeply miss my mother. Grandma only confuses me with her constant worrying, and I feel strange about all the attention she puts on my "bowel movements," as she calls them. No one speaks to me about what is happening to my mother or why she hasn't yet returned. I no longer believe the lies and put-offs. I begin to suspect every one around me is dishonest; I worry that my father is hurting my mother. I worry about the pain in my bowels. I feel nervous and insecure. I want to get away. I feel like I'm in hell.

Outside my grandmother's house is a lilac bush; it beckons to me with its cool, inviting shade. I find a little nook around the base where the branches make a secret cave so I can see out but no one can see me. I breathe in the sweet fragrance of the lilac flowers, and sit quietly feeling the earth under me. I am filled with a natural sense of peace, almost as if the lilac bush is a womb surrounding me with a motherly presence. I feel no fear here, and all the pressure of grandmother's world releases for a moment. I feel a deep sense of peace.

I am far too young to understand or conceive of Divine Mother energy at this time, but this first encounter with the Sacred Feminine presence in Nature impresses me deeply. In my body, heart, and soul, I both intuit and accept the authenticity of the experience, accepting it with a child's pure innocence. When my Grandma comes out into the yard looking for me, I sense that she is nervous and upset. She seems worried; she calls my name over and over. I ignore her, and allow the moment to pass without answering her call. After she leaves, I listen to the sound of the birds and bugs as the cool twilight engulfs me.

§ § §

A few weeks later, I awaken to the commotion of people chattering. I hear a sound that strikes deep to the core of my being, piercing my body and heart with its beauty—Mom! I crawl out of the bed and, rubbing my eyes, peer around the door.

She is back! At the sight of her sparkling eyes and smile, tears of joy spring to my eyes. I try to call out to her, but my throat is swollen with emotion. She is talking excitedly, but stops suddenly when she sees me. Her arms open wide and I finally feel my mother's embrace again. Our reunion is cut short when babbling adults demand her attention, asking question after question.

Mother has not come back alone. My little brother is with her, and a new baby brother. My dad is with her, too. I feel shy, shy and jealous of my mother's attention, wary of what my father might do. I feel uneasy, nervous, self-conscious, dissatisfied.

The mother I had waited for never did come home—someone else came instead. I am not happy and my mother can do nothing to appease me. She is surprised I still wet the bed and suck my thumb. My father is like a stranger on his best behavior. I don't feel comfortable with any of this and cannot help but sulk much of the *time. A fuming infant-dictator inside, I am constantly in a temper-tantrum. Any time I express my frustration and upset, I get punished.*

Like so many adult men, when I look back on what happened I wonder how I even survived. The pain of that child still lives in my body and mind. At three and four years old, I did not have the ability to deal with the situation, and there was no one mature and savvy enough in my world to see what was happening or what was needed. All the unbearable and confusing thoughts and feelings had nowhere to go but into my unconscious. All the moments of a small, bewildered boy, angry, tense, upset and desperate, had to be capped. I was like a steaming volcano. That's when I gave control of the reins to this unconscious inner child. My attitude toward others was literally, bent out of shape over and over again. My feelings about love, men, women, brothers, family, right and wrong, were influenced by those early events. My attitude toward getting what I want—or getting what I don't want, as the case may be—became deeply twisted and ingrained.

Feelings of impotence, in the face of something imposing on me—anger, rebellion, doubt, fear, resentment—all can be traced back to that time. So many reactive patterns that grew rampant within me began in response to those early events. Not until my thirties did I examine any of this. I had completely forgotten about what happened when I was young. When I first began to remember, I fell prey to feeling like a victim. It took a long time for me to see that my inner child was using my adult powers in unconscious and devastating ways.

It is late summer 1994, I am forty-seven, and have been away from my family of eighteen years for about six weeks. The initial intoxication of falling in love with a girl half my age has passed. Her presence in my life has been accompanied by experiences and energies in my body and emotions I never imagined possible. As the rapture and bliss of our early infatuation fades, the roller coaster ride takes a deep, plummeting dive.

I feel rejected, abandoned, and lonely. My girlfriend has gone away "to take some space and time out." I have not been without a relationship with a woman since I was eighteen. I feel insecure and fear this relationship might not last. My family is no support now; they will not have me back.

Inside, I seethe with rage. I want to control people, situations, even my own emotions, but I cannot. My usual arrogant stance is no defense. I'm in too deep to stay numb. I feel stupid and lost, like a little kid. I feel like a prisoner of circumstance. I'm forced to live off a friend's hospitality, helplessly waiting for my girlfriend to return. I feel like smoking (I am trying to quit) and being alone to think. I excuse myself from the chattering relatives and guests my friend has over for the weekend, and leave out the back door to sit on the porch. I walk outside and see a lilac bush.

Memories flood through me. For the first time in my adult life, I remember and feel the four-year-old me. A feeling of connection to this inner child goes deep into the center of my being. I am aware of my adult self, and at the same time, I am aware of the little kid inside me. I feel the kid lead me into the lilac bush and sit me down. I become as receptive as possible, and a tidal wave of memories washes over me. I am surprised to remember the feelings and circumstances that occurred back then so clearly. Even more surprising, I realize I had only remembered what fit the familiar, endless story about every one else being at fault when I don't get what I want.

Sitting under the lilac bush, I feel the kid inside me so close and so real I put my arms around him. I open my heart and embrace him with the love he so desperately needs. I console him, comfort him, and assure him that I, as an adult, will take care of him. Suddenly, I become aware that a lilac bush has once again brought me into contact with the Divine Mother, and that it is this connection with the Earth I am remembering along with the challenges I met as a child. I feel the energy of the lilac bush and the earth, and recognize them as a resource I want to tap into more. I sit in this realization for a while, feeling a sense of unity as energy flows tangibly between my body, mind, heart, and the Earth.

This strengthens me. The Divine Mother is working within me, helping me face my discernment of how I have acted foolishly. My passionate intoxicating affair with this young lady has led to disaster. And now, sitting under the lilac bush, I am able to evaluate the situation more clearly. I sit within the lilac womb again, led by spirit to use this space as a resource that can help me accept and learn my lessons. I can accept the reality of passion overpowering my judgment, stupidity clouding my choices to ignore my family, and blind selfishness destroying all I lived and worked so hard to build. I take a deep breath. The air is ripe with the fragrance of lilac. Calm, serene acceptance of even all this rejection of myself pervades past my wailing angst. The lesson is hard and deep: "When it comes to love, pay attention to the ones you already love, especially if passion tempts you to leave them."

On my fifty-seventh birthday, I was gifted a lilac bush by a very dear friend. It sits in a big pot on my porch, waiting for the day I will plant it in the earth I call "home." My inner work on this healing journey over the past decade has brought more and deeper awareness of my inner child, more contact with the feelings and attitudes that stem from the walled-off, unconscious, reactions of the immature me. Putting self-recrimination and judgment aside, I can relax and look at these emotional states through the eyes of maturity and experience. Rather than ignore, repress, or deny these childish reactions, I witness them with objective discernment, but no longer allow the inner child to have a free rein with my adult powers. That would be like letting a child play with atomic bombs, something I am tired of repeating in my life.

The process of awakening to consciousness, growing up, is like deciding to grow a plant to its full potential. For instance, I love Meyer Lemons. I might buy a small lemon tree, and bring it home in a container from the nursery. At first, the citrus plant is fine sitting in the yard and being watered every few days. As it grows, I realize it needs a bigger pot, or it may need to be planted in the ground where it will get the best exposure and right amount of sun. If I want the tree to bear fruit in a few years, I will do what is required to make sure it gets the best conditions.

The personality is like that; it is grown up in a container called a "family." Families, like nursery containers, are a great way to get a new shoot started, but they are also fantastic weavers of Maya, or illusion. Maya is the stuff of existence, seemingly solid and real, but at the quantum level far less so than we think. Maya is like a movie playing in the mind, the cinema of our karma plays out specific scripts, or lessons. Karma refers to the rules of the game, the cause and effect relationship between our true intent in the choices we make. As freewill beings dealing with the potent force of freewill energy, we either take responsibility for our actions or not. In so doing, we make a choice to be either conscious or unconscious. If we reject the truth and information of reality, and hold to conceptual, mental, and emotional tricks to keep us in the illusion, we sacrifice coming into contact with who and what we really are.

We are bound in illusion from the beginning, and we struggle to break free, using awareness and consciousness to realize who we are in the midst of it all. We discover our real self, who we always have been, through the practice of awareness, which leads to insight. Higher awareness dawns with the recognition that, "I am a being who has been forever and will be forever as are all other beings around me." In this realization, the temporary nature of everything becomes evident and no longer threatening. Everything in the universe is temporary, impermanent, the stuff of Maya. And yet, *the permanent eternal spirit behind all temporary manifestation can also be perceived—this is the perception that expands our horizon and leads to higher consciousness.*

Just as the sensory perceptions are always available for us to choose to use, the perception of higher consciousness is also a choice. All experiences are available to our intimate individual awareness; we can choose higher or lower aspects as our karmic lessons unfold. For example, we can have the experience of being depressed or the experience of bliss. We are going to have many experiences in our life, one at a time, or several at a time, because whatever we focus on is our choice. It's not like God is going to knock us on course, we're going to knock our self on course; God is the course.

When we care enough to give compassionately of ourselves, and to share what we have learned, we reinforce our own development. More than that, we set up an energy field that allows the next lesson in our process to come in. If we can be in the present moment while sharing, rather than pushing the thought, "You need to think about my agenda," then we can be totally available with all our resources to hear and respond with deep consideration and compassion. This allows us to channel our authentic power with a true healing focus. At the same time we set up the karma to receive similar help when we need it—help that does not exploit our plight and does not victimize us.

If we want to stop telling the tales that keep us feeling like a victim, we have to start by not victimizing our self or others any more. We *can* stop the movie when we see it as "the story." The brain won't do this on its own. Left to itself, it fires up all the chemicals it did when the incident we are remembering first occurred. *We cannot tell our story without totally recreating the experience of that story within our self. If we don't want to keep experiencing it, we can choose to quit telling our story.* We all did this when we got tired of blaming the cast-iron skillet for burning us and quit picking it up with our bare hands. When we've had it with our story of how we are a victim of the universal frying pan, we reach for real help. Thinking about being a victim, telling our self and everyone else how victimized we are, merely recreates the experience of being a victim. This is because we are paying attention to the victim's movie instead of our actual life.

We go where our attention is. Our experience is shaped by that to which we give attention. When I don't pay attention to what I agree to in business, as well as relationships, I often find I will be paying more than I think something is worth. This is a basic rule of reality most of us understand implicitly, and yet we live in denial and ignore the actual effect of our lazy or distracted attention. If we follow this thread, we can easily see that what causes most of our problems is stubborn or ignorant insistence on denying what we know. What we know is not paid attention to.

We are not speaking here about the normal conscious awareness that our personality wears like clothes to fit our mood. We are talking rather about a broader awareness that we as adults are capable of attaining. This expanded awareness sees more than just what the personality filters to fit its programmed agenda; it can hold a perspective of our self in relation to others that is not fooled by the appearances of duality.

This awareness is given to us freely and yet we so often throw it away. It is as if a homeless, starving man threw fresh food away in favor of what he could scavenge from the garbage can. The ways we disregard and override this awareness don't really make sense; but this awareness is present whether we choose to be conscious of it or not. It collects and compares all the sensory information and reflects on what we have experienced.

Like a bead, a single insight from our expanded awareness by itself does not amount to much, but strung together with others it makes life a beautiful work of art. Like a necklace, rosary, or japa, practicing and working with awareness, having moments of insight and awareness strung together over time, is more useful than a single bead. We actually wear all of what we've become aware. Even if we forget we are wearing a necklace, others still see it on us; our level of maturity and development is obvious. So too, awareness is always with us even if we forget.

Attention is the currency that allows us to have this awareness. When we are attentive, we become aware that we are more than our personality, our body, our lifetime, or our programming. We are aware of more information than just what the five physical senses bring us. We are aware that awareness itself is the energy field in which we live and breathe.

Our collective priority on Earth right now was beautifully summed up in the Assisi Decalogue. This historic coming together of the religions of the world to align on a set of principles that unites all religions in service of our collective well-being establishes a new paradigm. This is serious business that demands a serious approach. *To change on a massive level, the collective attitude of humanity must change.*

Growing up and outgrowing the inner child's reactivity is similar to politics in the wielding of power. The powers of an adult American are potentially unlimited in the world today, yet these powers are run by an infantile mental and emotional consciousness. This is obvious when we look at the metaphor of our elected leaders that "represent" us; their immature attitudes towards how to use adult, modern, state-of-the-art armaments are very toxic and physically dangerous to all people on the Earth. We are collectively responsible for handling the mega-Goliath superpower we have become, and that means it is time for humanity to grow up. Leadership is desperately needed; spiritually, emotionally, and mentally mature leaders must come to the fore.

We cannot afford to be unrealistic about what abuse of power can do in the nuclear age. The religious leaders of the world all agree with the Assisi Decalogue because they realize what abuse of political power can do today, and they refuse to allow religion to be a justification for political rationalizations about war. Experience and common sense, should caution us. If power can be abused, and a power-hungry individual steps into a position of power, he will abuse his power. The old admonition, "Power corrupts and absolute power corrupts absolutely," has never been more graphically demonstrated than by the power elite of our day.

How do we deal with the abuse of such enormous power? We grow into our authentic power and use it, each doing what we can where we are. Everybody who wrestles with these problems and overcomes them with higher consciousness, taps a deep well of authentic power we all have inside. One by one, and in groups, we share what our authentic source reveals to us; some through art and creativity, and others through healing and guidance. We stand at a fork in the road: will we achieve world harmony, or will all life on Earth be destroyed by ignorance and greed? Both are real possibilities but only one road can be chosen—world harmony is now equally possible as well as the traditional destruction and war syndrome. *The bottom line is that each of us must do what we can, now more than ever, to deal with our own ignorance and greed.*

Am I responsible for those who choose paths that are destructive to life on Earth? Yes! They must be curtailed immediately. This can be done without a war on terrorism. Our attention must be brought to bear on the more insidious evils that cause terrorism—namely, abuse of human rights and the environment. My challenge in this life has always been to find a way, without a gun (or a fist) to stop the bullies who not only have one but also choose to use it. Finding a peaceful way to deal with the anger I feel at the atrocities heaped upon others has been my lot in life. I have seen the abuses first-hand in some cases, others I have heard from eyewitnesses.

A lifestyle buoyed up by television and convenient shopping malls shields us from nuisances like genocide or ethnic abuse. We live in the land of the happy and clueless. *To truly take responsibility, we must recognize that only those able to respond are really responsible.* Here in America we have the freedom and resources to respond to the world situation. The ecological catastrophe is our responsibility. "Clean up your mess," may not have been our favorite childhood lesson, but if we don't get the lesson now it will most certainly prove fatal.

The good news is the solutions are emerging as quickly as the problems rise to the surface. We know what to do, and a powerful grassroots movement is growing up around the world. The Bioneers Conference is a movement and a trend that will not be stopped. We could be on alternative fuels within a few short years, especially if we redirect our efforts from oil wars to a battle that *can* be won—the fight for awareness over ignorance.

Our responsibility is first to the survival of the environment, because if we allow it to collapse we will go down as well. Reflective consciousness is now a collectively shared consciousness through communication and technology. In the face of species-extinction, the debates of religion, philosophy, morality, and ethics pale into oblivion compared to the really important issue of this evolutionary moment in history. Truly, it will be humanity's will that shapes the future; no other species has the ability or consciousness to do it.

So, what other control is there but authentic power? What other choice is there but to go within ourselves and find the unconscious tyrant that would have us destroy our very life and the ones we love, to bring that hidden child out into consciousness where, as adults, we can take care of those childlike concerns without being controlled by them. Ultimately, growing up and becoming mature means being responsible for our experience. Blame, shame, and judgment are reactions based on fear programs that a child cannot handle. *When we or anyone else use shame, blame, judgment, or fear, it is the inner child holding the reins to the adult's power.*

Today, we experience evolution maturing us in a process that involves conscious engineering of our future as twenty-first century humanity. That is why we feel the urge to find mature leadership, leadership that respects the safety of all we risk when we wield such potentially devastating power. Or more appropriately, we seek the inner leadership that can wisely do away with positions that could abuse such power in the first place. Maturity is not about age; it is about using common sense, and wisdom. There is no place in an enlightened age for the dangerous childishness that has ruled in ages past. We must apply everything we have learned as a collective, apply what we have learned from our long history and experience at war. That means we focus with common sense on what works, and learn how to fix what doesn't work.

In our relationships we cannot afford to allow the child in each of us to rule. When that child uses the atomic power of some intimacy—some shared, private secret—as a weapon to purposefully hurt, the betrayal of the trust can permanently break the relationship. Almost everyone has done this, and had it done to him or her. It is part of our growing up as kids, and part of our maturing as adults. When this happens in the relationships that matter to us the most—the ones we are deeply invested in—the loss can be catastrophic. When this happens internationally, as in shoving aside hard-earned peace accords and UN Council to wage an illegal war such as our government has done in Iraq, untold cost to human lives results. Trust in our leaders is destroyed in the process.

Evolution meets human consciousness now, within us, and everywhere in our world. It demands that we apply our human consciousness and our collective will to the survival of life on Earth. As a race, we are like an adolescent with one foot in the child's world, and one foot in the adult's. We have the ability to use our adult powers in a childish way. *The saving grace is that the collective consciousness of humanity is now growing up and reaching for wisdom, to the degree that each one of us is also doing so.*

Our future leaders must have the vision to inspire us to follow them because they walk their talk, and talk what they really know is true: this builds the trust necessary for the monumental changes humanity is undergoing now. Our own individual task is likewise, to walk our talk, and to know what we are talking about. This is what growing up is really all about.

9

SEX, LOVE, ANGER AND TRUTH

Poor man wanna be rich, rich man wanna be king
And a king ain't satisfied till he rules everything.
I wanna go out tonight, I wanna find out what I got
Well I believe in the love that you gave me,
I believe in the hope and I pray that some day
It may raise me above these
—BRUCE SPRINGSTEEN

I am about five years old. A little girl from the neighborhood has come over to play in my backyard, and we start gathering acorns that have fallen from a huge oak tree. She squats near the ground and turns up the front of her dress for a makeshift basket. When she stands up to proudly display how many acorns she has collected in her skirt, a cold, electric jolt goes through my body and I get the shock of my young life—she is not wearing underwear! I cannot believe what I am seeing.

Until this moment, I had never thought about the difference between the sexes. It never occurred to me that girls do not have a penis and I am stunned. I wince in pain, imagining how she might have removed it. This is the beginning of my conscious sexual identity.

Sex, sexual identity, orgasm, intercourse, and everything that comes to mind when we hear the word "sex" is not all there is to this great mystery. Sex is a universal principle, as fundamental to how the universe runs as wheels are to the movement of a car. Sex may not make the world go

131

around, but it is what brings us, and everything, into existence. As such, it is the greatest creative force in the world.

We humans are the only species that gets emotionally hung up about sex, and uses sex for the sake of pleasure. There are many differences between human sexuality and that of other mammals. Each of us is born in a body that is sexually programmed on many levels. We get biological programs, hormonal, cultural, and parental programs. We are influenced by friends, and shaped by our experiences. Males get a different program than females, and the emphasis is pre-ordained culturally for both genders.

I am four years old. I've been invited to a birthday party for Susie, a little girl I play with frequently. This is the first birthday party I have attended for someone outside my family. My mother takes me shopping for a present and encourages me to get a pretty ring for "the pretty girl." This seems like a good idea to me, so I say, "yes," innocent to the implications of a boy giving a girl such a gift.

When Susie begins opening the present, my mother and the other moms who are standing in the corner of the room start to giggle. When the girl sees there is a ring inside the wrapping, her eyes get big as she says, "ooh!" All the moms laugh and say strange things I don't understand. I feel embarrassed, awkward and confused. They speak in a way that makes no sense to my four-year-old mind, so I withdraw like a turtle into its shell, seeking a place to hide. Thankfully, Susie is just as naïve as I, and she saves me further embarrassment by jumping right into opening the next present. Later, the moms continue their coy teasing, and I wonder what I have done to deserve this odd form of attention that so bewilders me.

My father had a different approach, which deepened my understanding of the male role in life. When my father moved back into the family home, I got punished at his hand more and more frequently. I was five years old and was literally a captive audience during the lessons he taught me— quite emphatically—about how men act: they are loud, angry, violent, and threatening. Once in a while, under special circumstances, they are jovial.

I am sitting at the dinner table, terrified, but defiant. My father threatens me with violence if I don't eat the canned asparagus that I have left on my plate. With a fierce glare, he tells me that if I throw up again he will have to spank me hard. I keep my eyes lowered, stare at my plate, and pretend to chew. He watches me like a hawk and insists on seeing me take a bite of the asparagus. I gasp at the odor as nausea rises up inside me. My stomach refuses to co-operate and I throw up.

My father's reaction is instantaneous; his hand viciously slaps my face as he barks out insults. He calls me a piece of shit, and yells, "It is all in your head. You can keep from vomiting. You are doing that on purpose, you ungrateful little shit!"

My face stings and hurts to the bone. I feel humiliated, but hide my pain, holding back the tears as he threatens more violence if I cry. The pain in my head and the nausea in my stomach make no sense to me. This is a long way from Grandma's chocolate chip cookies.

My mother calls this fascist ritual at the dinner table "discipline." Like so many scenes I experienced over and over, I am told that, "Men do it for the good of their children."

As the oldest of three boys, I am always told I am responsible for the others. I try the authoritarian techniques my father has taught me, but when they are big enough, the two of them gang up on me. From then on, periods of fun and play are interspersed with a serious game of blame-and-be-blamed. Although much of the time we get along, when we don't, it is like a war. We yell, scream, fight, and try to seriously hurt each other at times.

In the decades after World War II, little was known about post-traumatic stress syndrome; the psychological after-effects of "the war to end all wars" went largely unattended. Many Baby Boomers were scarred by the unconscious, dysfunctional attempts of their parents to deal with the horrors of that great, unprecedented conflagration. Alcohol use and abuse was rampant in the post-prohibition generation that spawned the baby boom. Alcoholics Anonymous was just publishing its first book when the war started. By the time it ended 250,000 copies were in circulation. Ten years later 3.5 million copies had been printed. Today alcohol kills over 100,000 people in the US annually.

CHAPTER NINE

In my immediate family, my mother's brother, "Uncle Lug," was the only one to serve on active duty in the army. I don't know if he was on the front lines or not, but now, looking back, I'd say he definitely had post-traumatic stress syndrome. While I was growing up, he was drunk almost every time I saw him. His wife, who also served in the war as a nurse, was the only one who could keep up with his drinking. Whenever we had a family get-together, the two of them inevitably had a drunken, loud, and nasty fight. Their two sons, my cousins, were embarrassed and fearful around them, and always wanted to duck outside and play while the adults got drunk.

My mom's dad was a quiet drunk who would just nod his head and smile, but rarely speak. Aunt Dorothy was a controlled drinker who only let herself go so far, never really got drunk, but drank a brandy or two every night. Grandma loved her port and my mother held her own with a penchant for Chablis. My mother's brother-in-law, Al, married to her sister Loretta, was my "rich uncle"—a cowboy-type as opposed to a real cowboy. He always wore fancy boots, cowboy-cut suit jackets, shiny snap-button Western shirts, and leather braid ties with turquoise slides. Uncle Al, a successful businessman, drank more expensive hard liquor, the kind with fancy names and gaudy labels that came in sculpted, hand-painted bottles. He and my Aunt Loretta were never totally drunk, nor totally sober. Then there was Uncle Ed, my dad's brother, who visited us for a while when I was a teenager. He had just been divorced and was going through AA recovery programs. I never saw him again after he was arrested for drunk and disorderly conduct while partying with a bunch of winos downtown.

Watching my father and uncles get drunk, obnoxious, loud, and violent shaped my sexual identity in confusing and contradictory ways. Bottom line, the message was: male privilege is normal. Also implied was that alcohol use is a socially acceptable means for dealing with pain and stress, and a perfect lead-in for having a good time. It didn't make much sense to me as a boy (the hot toddy that Aunt Dorothy made me when I had a cold only put me to sleep), but the message was very clear: alcohol is a man's best friend and his most socially acceptable intoxicant.

The psycho-spiritual fallout of World War II was far-reaching, but largely overlooked or denied by the populace. In this country, we were told to be grateful that the destruction had not hit our homeland when the reports of poverty and desolation came back from Europe. Soldiers like Uncle Lug received no rehabilitation. As a people and a nation, we had little understanding of how to deal with the terror of going to war and then coming home to resume "normal life." Post-traumatic stress syndrome had not even been named yet. American troops witnessed and committed horrendous atrocities in that war. People came home with deeply scarred and wounded spirits. Many of them became sexually, violently, and emotionally abusive toward their children and spouses. The media and Madison Avenue found the war propaganda profitable however, and millions of us were encouraged to play war games at home.

When I was five, my mother bought me a Davy Crockett outfit, complete with coonskin hat. Dressed like a real frontiersman, I carried my cowboy guns with pride. With a roll of caps, I pretended to shoot and kill, roll-playing the hero like billions of other kids before me, playing like little kittens pretending to be the lion king. My emerging sexual identity formed around two principal realities: women do not have penises, and men punish and kill. Knowing that men kill reinforced and increased my fear of my father. I lived with the strong impression that I could die at his hand. After all, men were supposed to discipline the family, and it was okay for them to yell, insult, and hit women as well as children.

What I learned about women was simply this: they cannot be trusted and will turn on you in a heartbeat. My mother reinforced this on a regular basis by rallying my father to punish my two younger brothers and me when he came home from work or from a sales trip. He'd come in the door tired, hoping for a relaxing evening, but instead would find a house full of pandemonium. At her wit's end, my mother would demand that he discipline the three of us boys. While mother went over her list of complaints and accusations, my father would get enraged. He would roll up his sleeves, grab a belt, and command, "Who's first?" I remember trying to figure out which was better, getting hit first or last. My butt always felt the same.

Of course, this did not make us look forward to seeing our father. We learned to sneak around mom, but dad's physical terrorism was a constant source of distress. We learned to tell lies in order to survive just being a kid.

What did all this have to do with love? Of the mature, responsible love children need from their parents, we were lucky to get any at all.

The ability to give mature love is rare yet for humans. Most of us experience what the inner child thinks is love, and that has very little to do with *giving* and more to do with *getting*. Many of us had our child's innate expectation of being loved shattered by immature adults with the power to physically, emotionally, mentally, and sexually abuse us in their confusion about expressing love. Sex, love, and anger became so blurred into one intense emotional experience that the words themselves became nearly synonymous.

Indeed, emotions are not so much a mental as a physical reality. Our feeling-response to outer events registers on the body as good or bad, painful or pleasant. Emotions differ from physical sensations that are caused by sensual stimulation of the sensory organs. Emotions are associated with memories and judgments. As children, we begin with physical sensory stimulation, exploring our environment with all our senses and categorizing the information. Then we make a judgment that some of these sensations are very pleasurable and others are very painful. Then we activate our willpower; and choose to pursue pleasure and avoid pain. The process is so automatic that as a child we are not even conscious of it.

The human need for physical touch and affection is essential to human development. Children are aware of this only instinctively, like they are aware of being hungry. When the stomach signals the need for food, the child signals the primary caregivers upon whom it depends for survival. It is much the same with the hunger for affection. Affection, however, is not a commodity to be consumed like food. Affection is a feeling that transmits love; generated through human touch and heartfelt attention, it is an energy perceived by a different sense than just touch.

Getting and giving affection is as close as humans have come to a definition of love. Certainly, love is experienced mostly as a feeling, not a substance. Maybe that is why all the confusing feelings from childhood about the word "love" led to further confusing feelings as we passed through puberty and began to explore sex. The hormonal surges in our adolescent bodies were intoxicating and caused new altered states. The pursuit of these sensations led to the pleasurable experience of orgasm. Overwhelming as the experience was, we interpreted this ultimate expression of affection as indication that we must be in love.

Then we grew up, our bodies leveled out on the hormones, and we pursued sexual experiences with varying degrees of love. Boomers were the first generation to have access to birth control pills, the Playboy Philosophy, and "free love." Further influences included the feminist rights movement, the resurgence of goddess worship, and the gay rights movement. After over forty years of screwing around, one might think Boomers have it all figured out by now.

What is sex today? Is it really orgasm we seek? What does love have to do with it? Is swinging better than monogamy? What is this illusive thing called relationship? What is marriage anymore? Whose family has not been touched by divorce?

Tantra workshops abound, dating clubs and casual sex clubs network millions of people daily, relationship books are on the best-seller lists, and even same sex marriages are made legal. Polyamorous relationships defy monogamous fidelity and make the notion of cheating obsolete for some couples as an "open relationship" becomes their great experiment. Clearly, our definition of sex is not what it used to be. Even if millions practice only the type of conjugal sex prescribed by the Pope, still millions more spread AIDS through unsafe sexual explorations. Even sex-bending she-males are sought as prostitutes, and child pornography is eagerly marketed. And now the problem of human cloning has arrived. According to right-to-life legislation, human rights begin as soon as the brain begins to function inside the womb. A new dilemma arises: how do we define "human"?

Our humanness involves a body with the alchemical force of emotions and a reflective consciousness that includes free will. Consciousness is inherent in both the definition and experience of being human, but the human body translates various states of consciousness into neurochemical, biological releases of hormones, which facilitate and activate higher evolved brain functions. Science can now track the brain and other body systems during the traditional mystic state of deep meditation, proving that even this state of consciousness is physically translated into the body's experience. Whether or not other energies and senses, besides those of the body, are actually accessed in these meditative states, whatever happens is experienced in the human body. *The definition of the word "human" is the same as for "humanity"—it is "consciousness"—the totality of our thoughts and feelings.*

The mystical, paranormal, telepathic, psychic energies, as well as fantasy and imagination: all are meaningful for humans. But we are all familiar with the age-old questions, "What happens when the body dies? Is consciousness dead?" We do know this much: if our individual consciousness shares its knowledge with the rest of humanity, at least that much consciousness lives on past the individual's death. But the answer to the question of what happens to the individual's consciousness is still unknown to science. This leaves the ancient claims of mystics and spiritual visionaries as still-unproven theories. If their theories are true—and the string theory, quantum physics and zero-point-field explorations of the last few years seem to indicate they are—then humanity is about to tap into our greatest mystical experience of consciousness ever.

From the perspective of consciousness, religious pedagogy seems little more than a mental construction, conceived by humans in an attempt to understand the vast powers at play outside us. "It must be an external agent—God, Allah, Elohim, Shiva—that creates, judges, and then punishes or saves us." This is why we continue to complain, and petition God with prayer, instead of realizing God's "helping hand" works with and through our own hands. As long as humans see salvation as outside of our self, we do not take full responsibility for our experience.

So what is the truth about sex, love, consciousness and the human experience?

In all the history of evolution on Earth there has never been a force as physically powerful as the sexual energy between a man and a woman.

Human experience is evolution's state-of-the-art form. It is not separated from the fabric of evolution. It is evolution conscious of itself and light manifesting itself. There is no return, for evolution thrusts onward now more than ever through humanity.

The universe is here, there, inside, and in every atom, molecule, cell, and body. The energy of the universe is light, and moves energy through all forms. This magnetic, resonant energy of sex that attracts humans is not the pleasure-procreation aspect anymore. Evolution has no use for these boring things now; there are more exciting possibilities opening up.

This eternal now moment, which is the "omnipresence" talked about by many, consists of electro-magnetic frequencies of light, sound, and vibration, which conduct through alignment and resonance a power of infinite magnitude. This allows for exponential evolutionary growth of consciousness throughout the universe. This moment in evolution is the beginning of conscious unity of these energies through humanity. The unified power that comes when sexual energy is harnessed consciously as a resource is an unparalleled source point of omnipresence. Our human consciousness is just beginning to understand what is beyond pleasure and procreation when it comes to sex.

The intent of evolution is conscious union of these energies in all directions. The separation never existed, does not truly exist now, and never will. The separation is a *misperception*, experienced as separation from omnipresence, and experienced as individual consciousness anchored in a sexual body of either a man or a woman. The impulse of fusion is evolution's prime directive in sex. Evolution's intent, here and now in humanity, is to inspire the conscious and useful manner of evolving: not just to breed life, but to evolve consciousness in life—conscious fusion, not only for procreation but for co-creation as well. This is what the human body is, and this is how it can heal the wounds of separation between man and woman.

True unity of bodies, and true aligning of powers, results in a sexual energy between male and female bodies wherein life is experienced as a divine emanation of omnipresence. Encountered directly, this divine emanation changes everything. Sublime and exquisite sensations, pleasurable beyond orgasms, begin to stimulate the body, mind, and heart. The bliss of unity sharpens our awareness of others with compassion, it inspires us to do the best we can with all our talents to make others happy, it spurs us on to even deeper self-realization, and it opens us to the highest and most noble aspects of human love.

The love talked about in romantic moments is an expression of our feelings of affection for another. It can mean anything from the jealous insanity of a fatal attraction, to compulsive-obsessive co-dependency, to completely autonomous acceptance of the other. "Love" has no definitive meaning; it is a subjective term in its general usage. The relative personal experience of our individual lives is what infuses the word "love" with meaning. The definition and feeling state we think of as love changes over a lifetime. The pursuit of love and our individual developmental process of defining and redefining what love is for us is the thread that weaves the story of our relationships. We may think we know what someone else means when they say "I love you," but when our heart gets broken, "love" suddenly seems like a very dangerous word.

The human quest for union seeks fusion on the most intimate levels of our physical, mental, and emotional being. This quest, more than any other, reveals hidden problems we have avoided. Sharing of our secret, intimate, innermost self penetrates many levels of psyche, mind, and heart. Trust is the foundation at each of these levels. When trust is lacking and the beloved seems like the betrayer, the love we felt touches the meanness in us and we unleash our darkest parts, which we may have kept hidden, even from ourselves. Lies, silence, avoidance, pretense, manipulation— all the things we humans are capable of come up in our most intimate relationships so we can work them out. The love we do feel for the other comes because we respect the higher qualities we see them exhibit in their behavior. This respect easily opens to trust, and opens up the intimate terrain where we can come to know even more about the other.

When we are disappointed because our expectations are not met, the love we feel can suddenly turn to anger. Feeling upset about having shared intimacies with another, who then behaves in a way that pushes our buttons, is an indicator that we have buried some very vital history in our unconsciousness; history we need to face up to with awareness so we can clear the blocks to total, intimate fusion.

Anger becomes the lifelong companion for someone who does not accept what happened to them in the past and does not face that experience now with all the maturity and resources of the adult self. *When we accept responsibility for our experience, we accept our self and our experience without the overlay of judgment. Accepting that no one else is really responsible for what we are experiencing right now, means that if we want to experience something else, we make a list of all our options and strategies to achieve our goals.* Only the inner child thinks someone else should make that critical evaluation.

I am almost through the first draft of this book. I am at a place inside where the memories are simultaneous with my here-and-now experience. The feelings I follow seem to lead me here so I can experience the similarities of the circumstances and the emotions. All the memories of sexual betrayal flood through my brain and heart. I breathe heavily; my nervous tension threatens to erupt in anger.

The victim inside of me watches as the circumstances of each atrocity parade by the judge. It doesn't matter which woman I think about, the feeling is the same. I rage at the unfairness and deceit. I want to explode out of this prison of injustice, wall up my heart, and never have relationships again. I am hurt to the core. My trust for the other is totally destroyed. As far as I am concerned, it feels like a matter of life or death; fight-or-flight impulses kick in. I feel like punishing them for my distress. If I had a bullhorn, I would broadcast an S-O-S signal loud and far.

In some of my memories, I wail at the tempests hurling against the beachhead of my heart and curse the woman involved. In others, I remember the deep sadness that hurts beyond my limits of endurance. I cry now because I do not want to hurt anyone. I feel like giving up, and then I feel like retaliating. Each heartbreak gave me a gift I cannot help but appreciate: each woman showed me another side of love. The respect and affection I still feel for them is profound despite turbulent emotions, and memories of betrayed trust that knocked my heart senseless. Each time I come out of these emotional tailspins, I

CHAPTER NINE

am clearer about my boundaries, and have a better sense of how to set limits.

The pursuit of fusion starts when we reveal who we are to another. If the revealing process goes both ways, we then begin to define who the other is in relation to us, and to the world. Then, if we move deeper into an intimate connection, we define love for both of us. Anger, fear, excitement, anticipation, the luxurious pleasure in moments of feeling bonded to another and emotionally met: all mix together with the amazing, mysterious, energy of sexual attraction. And this leads to an exquisite unveiling, a path of self-realization that is always unfolding. What begins in truth-seeking, a process of sifting through all the words and actions we encounter in another, leads to understanding of self, other, and shared destiny, for better or worse. In every case, we have the opportunity to see more of who we are.

Truth is either absolute or relative. "All is one" would be an absolute truth. "I feel one with you" would be a relative truth. The first is eternally true and the second may only be transient. Even our identification with this body in this lifetime can be seen as relative. We are also able to experience other lifetimes in other bodies. Our connection with our eternal nature is an absolute truth. Our story, the daily drama we can so readily get caught up in, is temporary. The eternal and the temporary always co-exist. In any given moment, the eternal presence accepts the spiraling of life, which evolves through all temporary forms and experiences.

The pursuit of truth is the pursuit of ultimate love, complete fusion with fulfilled consciousness. But this hardly defines what most people call relationship. They say instead, "Just give me a good time." Full and honest awareness is rarely part of the initial pursuit. This is why most relationships fall apart. Bonds formed on the basis of unconscious expectations and projections lead to unhealthy attachments and dependencies. We confuse feeling loved with our ability to love. Over time, both our understanding of love and our goals for relationship go through tremendous, unforeseen change. Lovers we may have shut the door on in anger come back into our lives and become lasting friends. Someone we blamed in the past might turn out to be our greatest teacher.

142

Likewise, we could blame our social and political disappointments on the many villains of history and never take responsibility for what is happening in our relationship with the Earth. We could blame, shame, and guilt-trip the scapegoats, and send them off to be punished, but that would not solve the problems they may have created. No one person or political party is responsible for the state of the world today. The modern world is the result of the collective mistakes and consequential lessons of humanity. All the dictators, terrorists, and tyrants of the past are here inside each one of us, clamoring to be allowed off their leash. But so are the saints and the heroes; they reside in the deep heart of every human alive.

Integrity is about integrating truth into our daily lives. Without honesty, honor, and accountability, we cannot have integrity. Communication suffers, as does relationship. Separation can exist in each other's presence, as when lovers refuse to talk while living in the same house. But when abuse begins to get physical, like with violence and war, accountability is demanded. In the state of California, as well as many others, there is a domestic disturbance law that requires perpetrators of violence in the home to attend anger management classes. Do we require less for those who can wield the nuclear sword of war?

Back in the days of the Vietnam War, the term *credibility gap* was coined. In our current world we are experiencing a credibility gap between the wishes of our leaders and those of the people that is the size of the Grand Canyon.

Conscious fusion cannot happen in our world as long as we respond to violence with more and more lethal violence. A more intelligent, considered, and humane response is needed if we are to advance and not devolve. We need leaders who seek and heed the mature, experienced counsel of humanity's collective evolving mind. What we don't need are yahoos who rely on reptilian-brain behavior, cannot think for themselves, and have been programmed by the military-industrial complex that created them.

Imagine being married to someone who comes home one day and says, "I'm sending our kids overseas to murder some Iraqi folks. The kids might die, it's going to be very expensive and ugly, but don't worry about it." Then when you question him, he gets angry and demands that he be allowed to do this immediately or he will lock you and the kids in your rooms. On the political level, this is the type of blind patriarchal force we are presently in bed with.

An important lesson I learned in the co-dependent dance of recovery is that "it takes two to tango." When the other refuses to stop the co-dependent behavior, it is our choice to leave the abusive relationship or stay and suffer more abuse. So, it seems like time in our political relationship to get that divorce and marry some guy who will care for our kids and our future in more realistic and functional ways.

The similarity between our personal sex lives and what goes on in government is not a new metaphor; being screwed over in either arena has nothing to do with love. Love and sex are vitally important, a necessary and potentially beautiful part of life. Human misuse of sex in the form of rape and abuse is an expression of uncontrolled bestial lust. Real people are turned into things, objects, property, and possessions. War also diminishes human values, treating people as objects to be conquered.

Sex, love, truth, and anger weave together in our personal lives; they overlap and mingle to make a marvelous tapestry or hideous travesty. Individual histories are reflected in archetypal energy dynamics shared with the collective history of humanity. Love, anger, and truth are fundamental issues playing out on the personal and political levels that will determine the survival or extinction of our species. Humanity's preservation has all the power of evolution behind it. The time has come for this consideration to become a priority in each of our personal lives by our complete attentiveness to all that evolution now gives us as resources to use—intelligence, creativity, common sense, and love.

It is important that each of us find a way in our lives to share truth. This means cultivating the potential within ourselves, the ability we each possess to express and communicate truth and love, especially in relation to anger or sex. This is not easy, or simple, and takes a strong commitment with a focused will. It takes dealing with the unconscious loops and patterns that keep us stuck in anger, pain, and abuse. It requires more effort than most people are willing to generate. But the weight of past abuses, "the sins of the father," have gotten so heavy as to threaten to crush us. The Boomer generation is poised to take responsibility for our own pain and abuse, heal the wounds of the past, and find the techniques that work and allow us to transform personally and collectively.

Humanity is waking up. The bottom line is: will we wake up soon enough? The cause of our biggest problems and the root of all wars is a set of values that do not suit the moment. Self-centered in the extreme, these values reflect an infantile, or at best, adolescent consciousness. An infant must have its needs met at great cost to others. An adolescent must assert himself to differentiate. But in a world where the cost to others could cause our entire climate system to collapse, and where assertion could bring on nuclear winter, the infant and adolescent aspects of our cultural mindset must now grow into early adulthood. That means each individual sensing his or her relationship to the whole. Fortunately, the sixties spawned a generation of "cultural creatives" who have spent the past forty years developing a set of values that is more mature and attuned to the times. This progressive value system is both more enduring and endearing.

We are finding ways to communicate love rather than anger. We are discovering how to free ourselves of the sexist mentality and respect both sexes equally. We are learning how to discontinue the authoritarian abuse of children. Most of all, humanity is learning about truth—not just individual truth but the beautiful truth of interconnectedness that is shared with all creation. The principles of unity and interdependence, which have always and will always rule life, are now verified by science. The spiritual understanding of how these principles work is the task of human consciousness. The will to act with this awareness is a choice in each of us and cannot be forced. Ultimately, our free will is the determining factor—whether humanity survives itself or not is up to each of us.

The collective human experience parallels the individual experience now more than ever. It is the collective energy and individual energy we now recognize equally, and then act in accord with our mutual goal—species survival. *The more we process the transformation necessary on Earth through our own personal experiences, the more as humanity we are collectively able to do the same.* A circumspect, maturing viewpoint, individually applied, will harmonize our energies to solve the huge but hardly insurmountable global problems. At the same time, our personal lives will harmonize better in all our relationships. This is the real Heaven on Earth; the Word made flesh, the actual salvation of the world. The crown of creation is offered to us now, but each of us must accept it, empower it with our free will, and manifest it in our own lives and our world.

10
FREEDOM

Tolling for the rebel, tolling for the rake
Tolling for the luckless, the abandoned an' forsaked
Tolling for the outcast, burnin' constantly at stake
An' we gazed upon the chimes of freedom flashing.
—BOB DYLAN

Today, when I reflect on the women who have been part of my life, I can tell the truth about having used them. Although I do feel some guilt and sorrow, I also understand that I acted in an unconscious way that is not who I am now. I accept what is, forgive myself, and look honestly at what's true here and now. This helps me to see the paradox of the simultaneous existence of my human frailties and my eternal connection with the divine. Through experiencing both, I am able to apply authentic power and change in a way that builds healthy relationships with myself and everyone else.

When I think about my kids, I am aware, more than ever, of the damage I have done to my relationships with them. At times, facing this overwhelms me. I want to give them something, something that will be meaningful in their lives, something from my heart: but I fear they will only be interested in money. When I left the family for another woman all those years ago, I abandoned the family financially and that has become a thorn in my side. I assume my children hold it against me. When I try to think about all this realistically, I wrestle with my ego and guilt.

149

Truth be told, my ex-wife has supported the family since the divorce and she has never pressured me about it. I have many mixed feelings about this: shame of not getting regular jobs, appreciation for her help of allowing me to get on my feet, guilt for not helping her, pride in her ability to do what she has financially, helplessness about the past, and anxiety about the future.

I want to talk with her about our children's finances because they are now in college. I am surprised at how much confusion and emotional intensity I feel. To give them money feels like an ego trip, a way to manipulate them emotionally and try to win their favor. I struggle with this in my mind for weeks. When I finally gather sufficient courage to call my ex and open the conversation, I ask if we can talk about money and tell her I want to know what the kids need. She is clear and specific and tells me about each one of the kids, giving me a quick update. I feel many mixed emotions and must struggle to keep my mind clear and unconfused.

While we are talking on the phone, my girlfriend drives up to the garage, and I get a jittery feeling in my solar plexus. I am nervous; I anticipate a possible problem. I wonder if she will act like so many other women in my life and be jealously suspicious about me talking to my former wife. The memories of such unwarranted frustrations in my relationships brings up intensely confusing emotions in my body.

I try to stay present and engaged in the phone conversation; but, as my girlfriend comes into the room, I feel perplexed and standoffish. She looks at me and nods at the phone as if to ask, "Who are you talking to?" I mouth the name of my ex. She hovers around me a little too long for my comfort, then leaves the room.

Feeling awkward and nervous, I abruptly finish the conversation with my ex, and sit for a while composing my feelings. In anticipation of an emotional upset with my girlfriend, I center myself with meditation-style breathing. When I feel calm and ready, I go out to the kitchen.

She looks confused and avoids eye contact with me initially, but as we start talking, she looks hard into my eyes. She says she is picking up a strange vibe about all this and I immediately feel on the defensive. I am very confused about my feelings and resent her calling them "strange." As she begins to accuse me of ulterior motives for not immediately and clearly answering her, I find myself getting angry.

I ask for space, and explain that I need to understand my feelings and sort them out before discussing the matter with her. She gets frustrated and says, "You'll pay for this," then stomps off with an angry look on her face. Now I feel deeply frustrated and more confused. I want to wail at her, but decide to avoid further trouble.

§ § §

The next day, I become very concerned that she might be angry enough to steal the supply of cash I keep in a safe place for emergencies. I feel it in my bones—she is going to rip me off. Although very aware that my hyper-vigilance about money has more to do with past betrayals than the level of trust in my current relationship, I decide to cover my ass and move the cash. I'm very aware of the fear that is driving me and can feel the compulsive urgency and anxiety behind my actions as I furtively hurry to my cash supply and move it to another safe place.

While this is happening, the eternal part of me watches without fear, learning from my obsessive-compulsive behavior. This is very new. In the past, I functioned blindly without the presence of what many spiritual teachers refer to as "the witness." Now I feel the difference as I watch my emotions play their tune rationalizing my behavior. Like when I hear the soundtrack of a movie and feel the emotions rise in my body, if I cover my ears the movie doesn't affect me the same. The witness helps me see from a perspective that is unbiased by emotion or fear.

§ § §

Two days later, I check on the cash supply and find that it is gone. My girlfriend found the new hiding place.

I am hot and seething with rage. I want to get mean and nasty. But the work I am doing on my path of self-realization makes me look at things in a different way now. I am able to recognize that the missing cash is not a matter of life or death. I am able to connect the dots and understand my impulses in the moment, and I know that I am responsible for what is happening. All of this puts a very different spin on what my choices are. I don't have to go off half-cocked and make an even bigger mess of the situation by exploding in a rage. In fact, part of me is deeply amused that she is playing this power game with the money. I decide to not let on that I know it is gone, and see what happens.

§ § §

A few days later, my girlfriend and I are in San Francisco for a rally protesting the one-year anniversary of the start of the bombing in Iraq. Our country is still at war; American kids placed in harm's way are dying over there. No weapons of mass destruction have been found, and it is clear that the Bush Administration deceived the nation in order to justify the invasion. Our troops are meeting more and more resistance, and stability in Iraq seems unlikely in the foreseeable future.

The weather in San Francisco is perfect for a march in the streets; the people again stage a massive rally. Photos and reports from the Middle East depict terrible human suffering from the war. There are leaflets and flyers being passed around. A stage has been set up at Justin Herman Plaza and one speaker after another steps up to the microphone to report on government deceit and the veiled intentions behind the war. Young anarchists, with their faces covered and dressed in black, yell at the cops. It occurs to me that the city could be in revolution soon.

A year of war and the real problems in our country are discussed in the streets. When does the government listen? The constitution refers to "peaceful assembly for redress of grievances." This implies the government ought to seriously consider the grievances of the people. Instead, they are disregarded by a president who, when asked if the nation-wide peace rallies mean anything to him, says, "I don't let special interest groups influence my decisions." The only special interest that unifies the diverse mixture of people at this rally is the desire for peace and an end to war.

It is a nice day to be together, and my girlfriend seems more relaxed with me as we walk around the city. By the time we get home, the issues between us seem less heavy and we are able to talk. Eventually, she admits, "By the way, I moved the money."

Calmly I ask, "What was your intention in doing that?"

"To make you have to come to me for the money so you would know how it feels."

I think this over, and tell her I feel very sad that she would take my hard-earned money, especially since she knows how much similar betrayals have pained me in the past. She is confused and so am I. We go to bed in separate rooms.

§ § §

Throughout the next few weeks, I search within myself for understanding, hoping to clear up my confusion. Over and over again, I am brought to the feet of the infant tyrant within me who hides in my unconscious. I see how intimacy must be balanced on the sexual, emotional, and mental levels of a relationship. The situation forces me to look at my tendency to avoid emotional intimacy and focus instead on sexual intimacy. I see the imbalance this has caused in my relationships in the past, and I see how it is pushing my present relationship off-center. Even though my sexual intimacies are wonderful for the most part, my mental and emotional levels of intimacy are intensely disappointing.

I begin to see the pattern, but fall into it again by not communicating my honest feelings to my girlfriend about the money she has taken. I realize the underlying rationale is that I fear her anger and want to avoid confrontation. Her tendency to take everything personally has me walking around the house as if the floor were covered with rice paper. Suddenly I realize that my tendency is to personalize everything, too. In a strange epiphany, I recognize that I am blaming and criticizing her for things I do. Blaming her allows me to maintain the appearance of being the nice guy in my mind's eye—such a farce! When I am mean, it is far from nice. "But I am less mean than her," my rationalizing voice says, "that gives me the right to act mean once in awhile." The absurdity of this argument reveals a deeper truth: I create situations with her that confuse both of us because I am in denial about the imbalance on the emotional and mental levels of intimacy. I want the extreme bliss of sexual intimacy and ignore or avoid clashing on the mental and emotional level in hopes that things will work themselves out.

More and more I come to recognize what now seems obvious: I cannot ignore any of the three essential aspects of my relationship — sexual, mental, or emotional. Each is vitally important to the health of the relationship. Denying this plays havoc with my life.

I can no longer ignore the truth; I must speak and act in alignment with this new understanding and be as honest as I can. Fear and doubt block the expression of truth. I must relinquish the fear and the doubt in my communications with others. No more hidden agendas, no more manipulations. Pure, open, honest expression of self. No defending, no obsessing. Clear, untouchable freedom. Only obstacles can make us strong enough to claim this knowledge of self. I give thanks for every endeavor, work, labor, and effort that has brought this to be. Freedom really only comes to those who earn it by struggling within themselves and wrenching it from the hands of the infant tyrant who refuses to let us fly free.

Reflecting on these dynamics as they play out in the larger world, it is relatively easy to see that the tyrants of history are not much different from the infant tyrant inside each of us. From this perspective, a despot could be defined as a ruler who lacks the mental and emotional maturity to wield power in a considerate, safe and noble manner. The catastrophes of war are blatant proof that the stage we have reached in our social-political evolution is yet hellishly brutal. Hitler, Napoleon, and all the famous bullies of history were geniuses in some ways; but they were dysfunctional when it came to using power. Abuse of power is still the norm. Civilizations rise and fall by the sword and the warhead.

History may repeat itself, but at some point—perhaps now—we must ask the tough question: is war and force really useful anymore? One would think the holocaust ovens of Nazi Germany and the atomic bombs dropped on Hiroshima and Nagasaki were enough to wake us up. But no, since Hitler's defeat, we've seen Stalin murder millions, and other bullies get away with massive murder under the guise of national security. Fascist dictators and puppet democracies have slaughtered millions throughout the world. Sanctioned by the archaic idea of individual national sovereignty, despots have claimed the right to do whatever they want in their countries and to invade and attack others as Saddam did with his invasion of Kuwait and the US with the invasion of Iraq. Billions of humans accept this as human nature, and an unavoidable aspect of reality. Why? What part of it makes sense in this modern day and age?

The work of maturing mentally and emotionally is largely in the pursuit of understanding, which leads to the development of aspects of self that have remained unconscious, reactive, and governed by societal, familial, and cultural programs. *The hidden controller inside each of us gets away with childish terrorism precisely because it is hidden.* Like a puppet master who pulls our strings, it hides in the unconscious directing the charade. The puppet master wields his power to create an illusion of invulnerability, staying safe behind the curtain. But like the Wizard of Oz, once the all-powerful one is revealed as a scared little man playing tyrant from behind a curtain, he no longer has power over us. In the movie version, the Wizard begins then to use authentic power, giving Dorothy and her friends resources that really work for them: a heart, courage, and a brain. This helps her use the magic shoes, which can take her back to where she was when she was blown away in a mighty wind to Oz—home with the people she loves most.

In the simple process of revealing and accepting the truth, the tyrant transforms into a true king. He loses his forcing-current power and gains authentic power. Once we open our awareness and take the high road to self-knowledge, opportunities for growth appear all around us. Rather than "modifying behavior" according to some external measure of right and wrong, we evolve new behavior aligned with our deeper understanding. These changes emerge from an *internal* ethical awareness that guides as surely as any compass.

This is internal, authentic freedom as opposed to the illusory freedom that is won with force. One is eternal; the other is temporary. As children, we began to impose limitations upon the free expression of our authentic, deepest self. We chose attitudes and patterns that denied our freedom, not consciously, but, by allowing the inner child to choose, we gave our subconscious the control. We began to see freedom as something outside of us that could be obtained or attained. We forgot we are freedom itself. With our authentic power we can remember we are free and thus free ourselves from our own tyranny.

The Boomer generation has a clear shot at freedom because our ancestors lived and died for freedom. I did not get free on my own; real humans actually died so that freedom could evolve. People laid down their lives to help others become free. They fought the oppressors, the tyrants, the emperors, and kings who would enslave them. They went into the most desperate situations knowing they would die, but hoping that it would let others live in freedom. They weren't thinking about democracy, they were thinking about mom and the kids. They were on the front lines to protect the lives and freedoms of the humans closest to their hearts. The source of true freedom within gave them the strength and the power to fight for freedom on Earth. The result of their efforts is the possibility of freedom being won that now stretches everywhere.

The freedom humans have today on the external level is far beyond the most awesome imaginings of the past. The reach and grasp of humanity has increased exponentially on the inner dimension as well. The freedom talked about by Christ, and all true masters and teachers throughout time, is available everywhere. Millions now share secret teachings, techniques, information, and attitudes formerly hidden in mystical occult schools. New teachings appropriate to our times, as well as new forms of relationship techniques and new attitudes, combine with ancient knowledge to reveal whole new options. Fueled by evolution's prime directive, humanity seeks new solutions to old problems. *Freedom and free will are propelled by our consideration of every option of which we are aware.*

Freedom is not really won by a gun. Defending freedom is not a matter of rallying the troops anymore. "We have met the enemy and it is us." Defending freedom by imposing slavery is an absurd contradiction. Protecting freedom requires diligent attention to all levels of awareness. Every thought, every word, every emotion, everything that we do and be determines the degree to which we truly live free. The monumental and exhilarating task of finding freedom is here for those who see and devote themselves to bringing the possibility into reality. Freedom is not handed to anyone; it is won—championed, in fact—by awareness, courage, and persistence.

Those who know this do what the heart and spirit tell us now, this moment—now, now, now. There is no place to go, no place to hide, no place safe enough, no place to avoid the impending environmental collapse, no one to talk into or out of our point of view. There is no one here but us— those who think deeply about life, spirit, and the moment that is upon all humanity—we are all comrades.

I have spoken here about freedom, love, light, bliss, awareness, eternity, divinity, the Self, the center, the source, peace, and oneness. These are all words that describe different aspects of the inherent unity of existence. There is no one word for this and so we use many. Taken all together, these ways of seeing our selves get us closer and closer to the truth. This place inside of us is all these things and more. It exists forever just behind, or underneath, the fabric of our lives. It is always accessible. What we call peace, love, bliss, is always available to be consciously brought into our day-to-day awareness. It is always a choice—*I* must make the choice—to focus on this aspect of my self. Yet the choice is not always easy; I still get lost in moments of confusion. When I relax my doubts, fears, and anger, I find myself experiencing this source of all peace.

Again and again, however, I come back to this connection with the Self. It is the only work that feels really worthwhile. I know now that this eternal resource is always present. I reach within to take this resource in hand and relax into acceptance of what my life really is. I choose to act without fear or doubt. I boldly proclaim a new day upon the Earth, the end of fear.

I propose that humanity is birthing the collective Human Being, and our generation is experiencing the labor pains of this birth. Bringing awareness to the process, we become midwives to the new humanity. We tune in, facilitate, and co-create with all life, finding that place inside where we can see all humanity as one. Then we apply all our talents and inspirations to acknowledge this change in our world. We voice and disseminate all we can, being as artful, beautiful, graceful, and entertaining as possible. Opening up, we listen, ask questions, invite and require accountability. We peacefully say "No" to war and murder. We walk our talk and insist on consideration of all possible alternatives. Most importantly, we take on our own psyche and weed out those unconscious, immature ways of being we are asking our leaders to redress. We take personal responsibility and balance our emotional and mental lives, examine our desire for more and more pleasure, our desire to inflict pain and punish. We must demand, in both our personal lives and in our political leadership, that communication become truthful, honest, and without secret agendas or hidden covert operations.

To do these things in our lives, and in our relationships, is to participate in the evolution of the higher potential of humanity. Boomers are the pioneers in this process, having come from abuse and co-dependency to challenge our own values as well as the values of our parents. As we change and emanate the vibration and frequency of truth, our world is equally challenged to keep up with us. All around us, our changes are reflected in everything else. When enough folks begin to live the new way, the dinosaur world of might-is-right will fade away.

Metaphorically, terrorism is our collective human terror of the unknown. Feeling only fear and doubt, fight-or-flight, we attack or defend to get our way. But terrorism claims that there is an invisible enemy, hidden amongst us with a suicidal intention of destruction. *An unknown secret power that can destroy us can only be dealt with if it is known.* Now is the time to take our individual and collective human experience about this unconscious power and bring it into our awareness. The inner child of humanity has been unconsciously controlling our behavior. Awareness begins the process that leads to an astounding discovery: we have within us the resources and intelligence to both deal with the past and design a brand new future.

Publicly silencing, killing, or imprisoning the opposition is how tyrants respond to free, peaceful people. The tyrant cannot afford public opposition or public awareness of real agendas. Secret police, secret plans, and secret weapons are used in secret ways to maintain control. Opposition is sabotaged or assassinated. The Inquisition blessed these techniques as legal. This immature wielding of power by churches and governments is recorded in history. The terrorist trained by the US government, who terrorizes us later, is the same tyrant that never grew up. Repressed tyrants just bide their time and wait for the opportunity to impose tyranny on everyone. In this way, humanity's inner child has held the reins of tyranny.

So, as I deal with my childish bully-boss inside, and I watch the childish bully-leaders of the world addressing these issues of power, I see many similarities. It is easy to succumb to secrecy, not revealing our true intentions out of fear of being censored, forbidden, or punished. It is easy to point the finger of blame and then rally expert testimony to back it up. It is easy to be a bully. What is really hard is dealing with a bully without turning into one. The epic Lord of the Rings exemplifies this beautifully through the metaphor of the ring. We must take the ring of power, which "in the darkness binds," back to its source: fear. Facing our deepest hidden fears disempowers the darkness and brings the light of truth to the fore. We evolve the capacity to discern and everything changes. This is transformation.

The answers are not found in following a specific, pre-determined course, but in facing the truth about our reactive patterns and deciding to change. The default programs that have us acting out fear, blame, shame, and rage no longer serve us. When we refrain from behaviors that block the free and honest expression of our true self, we are refreshed. The unthreatened, open manner that naturally results can solve every problem.

I am an eternal optimist. I refuse to buy into doomsday fears and apocalyptical futures. I believe the emerging humanity is the ultimate merger of spirit and matter, the marriage of Earth and Heaven. I believe the evolution of this consciousness is beyond destruction, and I point to its trillions of years of painstaking, intricate manifestation. I know, without a doubt, that evolution moves me, as well as through me; it is the

CHAPTER TEN

music that inspires me to dance out of the shadow of tyranny and into the light of freedom.

EPILOGUE

After reading through this book with the question in my mind, "What key points am I making here about the specific changes humanity must undertake now to get through this planetary crisis?" I have outlined below the main ones I touch upon in the book.

1) Immediate international application of all the rights defined in "The United Nations' Bill of Human Rights" This is the most important step toward a world free of war, violence, abuse, and exploitation. This is absolutely neccesary for the rest of these points, which follow, to be implemented.

   a. Our world government must consist of nation-states united in a consensus democracy, based on a constitution that outlaws war, sexual and child abuse, national tyrants, and environmental pollution.

   b. Consensus democracy must replace "majority rule" or authoritarian processes.

   c. Positions of concentrated power that can be abused must be eliminated. Both politically and economicly, this is essential in order to cease the abuse and exploitation of all nations.

   d. No abuse of persons. No child abuse, no spouse abuse, no political or ethnic abuse.

   e. Historical accountability of the facts. No mental tyranny through censorship or control of information.

2) The next most important key to begin with is that war and violence must be universally outlawed and all preparations for war must cease.

   a. No testing of nuclear or biological weapons,

   b. no manufacture or research of new weapons,

   c. and the immediate disarmament of all existing weapons of mass destruction.

3) Number one priority for all life on Earth is that humanity clean up our relationship with the planet. This means:

   a. We immediately adopt non-toxic, non-polluting, appropriate technologies for our ecological health.

    b. All use of limited natural resources on the planet must be collectively decided by all nations.

    c. Carbon emissions must be targeted especially.

    d. Clean energy systems must be subsidized immediately.

    e. Humans must recognize our connection and participation in the energy of divinity, evolution, the Earth and the sun, our environment, as well as our attitudes and thoughts. This is the key to the shift in perception we need to solve our global problems.

4) Tolerance and respect for diversity must become an essential part of our global atttitude.

    a. It must be celebrated, encouraged, honored, and memorialized.

    b. Religious intolerance will not be tolerated.

    c. Worldwide religious tolerance at the same time "cult awareness" techniques must be taught to balance religious fanaticism and holy war frenzy with our modern world's needs to survive.

5) Worldwide elementary and secondary educational systems must include training and classes in:

    a. Nonviolent communication

    b. Listening skills

    c. Identifying and communicating feelings

    d. Problem solving

    e. Conflict resolution

    f. Options and strategy developement and recognition skills

    g. Consensus facilitation

    h. Anger management

    i. Meditation

    j. Relationship skills

    k. There must be pro-active changes in educational institutions and media corporations that encourage non-judgemental attitudes.

6) Free therapy and rehabilitation for all abuse victims, which includes those who suffer from post-taumatic stress due to war and violence. Free therapy for all military veterans.

7) Reorganization of all judicial criteria:

    a. on an "only if absolutely necessary" basis of violent crimes that have victims,

    b. and that appropriately differentiates between "punishment" and "rehabilitation" in sentencing;

    c. and have most judicial proceedings aimed at dealing with governmental and environmental criminals who are abusing all our human rights as outlined in the UN document on rights already mentioned.

    d. Also limits of per capita percentages for prison populations,

    e. as well as complete reform of all prison systems in order to cease abusive and degrading practices.

    f. Alcohol, drugs, tobacco industries must be accountable for the media advertising they do as well as have third party watchdogs monitoring the safe use of their products (even under doctors' supervision).

8) All people must have freedom from government and business intrusion,

    a. both personally in the privacy of their home and mentally from any tyranny or "chilling" effects.

    b. The human body must not be used as a witness against the person except in only the most severe of capital crimes.

        i. No use of any part of the body may be demanded by employment or social services.

        ii. No DNA, blood, or urine testing may be demanded by govenments or businesses for the purposes of tracking rehabilitation progress, or present and past crimes of citizens not charged with capital crimes.

9) International economics needs to change:

    a. No gross national production.

    b. No quarterly or yearly profits neccesary.

c. People without jobs can get free schooling.

d. Criminals can have sentences reduced through school and rehabilitation.

e. Welfare reform should be based on the premise that our world is better when we help our citizens heal, educate, rehabilitate, support their children and elderly, and become contributing members of society.

f. An international health care plan must be made available to all people irregardless of their ability to pay. This should include their choice as to medical treatment and preventative health maintenance too.

g. International acceptance of hemp as the number one natural renewable resource. This is essential for the development of hemp's ability to replace wood and oil, and to stop deforestation and petroleum pollution.

h. US tax reform:

   i. Contributions (e.g. 10% for the poor, 25% for the rich) to government projects of the individual's choice.

   ii. Sovereign citizens are exempt but also get no benefits.

   iii. Corporate taxes must fund environmental protection and watchdog organizations as well as employees' health care and retirement benefits.

10) There must be an international freedom of information which is:

a. Accurate and truthful.

b. Accessible to all.

c. Not controlled by corporate or special interest group monopolies.

d. Based on "the right to know" not the old "need to know" basis. (Today we all *need* to know.)

e. No government or corporate media advertising survellance or intrusion upon citizen's privacy.

f. Complete government accountability by third party recording archivists.

g. International free Internet access without political censorship must be made available

HUMANITY'S EMERGING CODE OF ETHICS:

THE NEW CODE OF CHIVALRY

After organizing the previous points, I see a code of ethics that can represent these goals. Like the chivalry of old, these guiding principles can help us address the "Might is right" energies on our planet today. I am putting them here as a focal point for discussion. There is nothing complete or set in stone here, these are merely considerations for each of us to take inside and find the way they apply in our lives. Integrity is the key here, integrating knowledge into our behavior and attitudes. Meditate on these elements of this evolving code and add your own too.

1. Unity/Oneness
2. Compassion/Nonviolence
3. Earth-Relationship/Responsibility
4. Tolerance/Respect for Diversity
5. Acceptance/Non-judgmentalness
6. Clear and Honest Communication—Listen/Speak
7. Fairness/Justice
8. Freedom/Non-tyrannical Attitudes and Behavior
9. Equality/Balance
10. Truth/Accountability

In essence these are the tools we can build a new world with. These are the seeds we can plant in our own life and nourish with our total and complete authentic power. These are the principles of life and the proofs of love. We can use these guidelines as the masters, like Jesus, have given them to us. By applying this new code of chivalry, we can love God, and love our neighbor as our self. For truly this is the heart of all religious commandments and the goal of all spiritual attainment: love!

ENDNOTES

1. De Chardin, Teilhard, *The Future of Man* (New York: Omega), p. 140.

2. Pierrakos, Eva, *Pathwork Lecture 120* (New York: Pathwork), p. 4.

3. Pierrakos, Eva, *Pathwork Lecture 120* (New York: Pathwork), p. 5.

4. See Bibliography for web link to read this PDF document in its entirety at your leisure.

5. Brzezinski, Zbigniew, *Out of Control* (New York: Touchstone, 1993).

6. Proverbs 13:24, "He that spareth the rod hateth his son: but he that loveth him chasteneth him betimes."

7. Pierrakos, Eva, *The Pathwork of Self-Transformation* (New York: Bantam, 1990), p. 138-9.

8. Herer, Jack, *The Emperor Wears No Clothes* (Ah Ha, 1998).

9. Ibid.

10. Rose, Philip, *Which One's Pink?* (Collector's Guide, 1998).

11. Read this document in the Bibliography.

12. Read this document in the Bibliography.

SELECTIVE BIBLIOGRAPHY

The teachers, experts, authorities, and sources for material in this book come from a lifetime of study on the spiritual path and being a visionary activist. I want to include here the books and people I was most influenced by, not only as basic references I used in writing this but as the main influences on my life. Each one of these sources is genuine and profound, they touch the core of my being. I am eternally grateful to the part of humanity that has made these works available, this is the real stuff, the culmination of human evolution at this time.

Each and every one of these references is the tip of the iceberg, beneath the surface is the hidden mountain of knowledge they come from, the collective human information pool. These are the people and books that I consider to be integrally involved in the new consciousness humanity is entering. These are not books I dug up to prove my theories, they are books that shaped and influenced me. You may read them all and come to different conclusions than I, but the influence upon our collective human mind by these sources is undeniable.

There are so many others that I could have mentioned but I am keeping this to just the most important and powerful that deal with the theme of this book.

Also, I am including here my website and email address so that if you are interested in dialoguing with me about the material in this book you can contact me at: Neriah@NeriahLothamer.com

Thank you for sharing this with me.

EVA PIERRAKOS AND PATHWORK

I am starting this selective bibliography with Eva Pierrakos, who, from 1950 till her death in 1979, channelled a series of 250-plus lectures focused on personal transformation. This is *the* most important resource for anyone looking for tools of self-realization which actually work. Called simply "Pathwork," this system is based on getting to being present in the now, by dealing with the unconscious past which is keeping us from it. The Pathwork however is only for those who are really serious about their self-realisation, as those who are not ready find. If you *are* seriously ready for practical techniques that produce results and require no more than your enquiring mind and focused will, then check out the Pathwork foundation online at: http//www.pathwork.org/. After you browse whatever you are curious about the organisation, then click on the 'lectures' tab in the menu button bar. There you will find all the lectures, as they were recorded, transcribed into separate PDF files that easily download for free to your computer, to be viewed or printed when you wish.

For more materials, they have available a few of the lectures on tape if you want to hear Eva speaking the lectures, and several books. The first two I recommend are *The Pathwork of Self-Transformation* and *Creating Union*, both available from the website and published by the Pathwork Press. The first one really gives the essentials of the Pathwork and will help you get some of the techniques working for you. *Creating Union* is more challenging and fulfilling I found, mostly because of the focus on relationship. The lectures on the *New Age Marriage* and *The Forces of Eros, Love, and Sexuality* are the pathwork lectures I first read when I stumbled upon the website searching for something else. They are also the ones I still read over and over again, as they reveal the most powerful tools for self-realisation especially in the most intimate relationships. Anyone who thinks they know what sex is all about, or love, or eros, or union; then they need to read these two lectures at least, and learn a new way of looking at these forces in our lives.

Pathwork has many communities and learning centers as well as regular workshops; but what is really different, they also have a "helper" program for those who want more personal help on their path than they can get out of the lectures. I have enlisted the aid of a Pathwork helper and find it more powerful than all the therapy, counselling, and teachers I have had. Pathwork helpers can be contacted via email or phone numbers available on the web at: www3.sympatico.ca/roddy.duchesne/reg_descrip.htm.

For the more professional, Eva's husband, John Pierrakos, developed "Core Energetics" which has incorporated much of the Pathwork into a system of techniques for therapists. Information on John Pierrakos, his books, and Core Energetics is available online at: www. coreenergeticinstitute.com.

THE TEACHINGS OF RAMANA MAHARSHI AND PAPAJI H. W. L. POONJA

As far as I am concerned, the teachings of Ramana Maharshi are the most valuable and essential resources in the realm of spiritual or mystical truth-seeking available now. Ramana was called by many "the greatest sage of the twentieth century." He never left Mount Arunachala after his samadhi there at eighteen years old. He lived there simply, with a beggar bowl and a loin cloth, until his death in 1950 at the age of seventy. Ramana's teachings involve a new technique in Eastern mysticism—self inquiry which continually asks, "Who am I?" It is a non-system which is based on being absolutely truthful with oneself.

I highly recommend all of the books which have his own words in them and any of the many written about him. To access information about Ramana and his books go online to:

www.realization.org/page/topics/ramana.htm.

Books can easily be found at Amazon.com by typing his name in the search field as well. I also recommend the videos about him which include one narrated by Ram Dass. The videos show rare footage of this remarkable saint and give an overview of his teachings.

Papaji H. W. L. Poonja was a devoted disciple of Ramana Maharshi and, I believe, spoke more eloquently about the teachings of his guru than anyone has. In fact, I consider Papaji the word-wizard of all time. His ability to poetically and powerfully present the teachings of self-inquiry are beyond all the human attempts in history to describe the mystical truths. His disciples are many, but he passed in 1997 at the age of 87 and thankfully was tape recorded by them, so that there are many of his talks in print now. The biggest and best is *What Is Truth?* The shortest, and most read over and over by me, is *This* which is composed of special selections from "What Is Truth?"

I find the words of Papaji to be my spiritual resource during the darkest nights of my soul, they so sweetly bring me again and again to know truly who I am. More than poetry, philosophy, mysticism, or personal growth techniques, the words of Papaji are a reality that roars through me as I read them, roars of truth, roars like a lion. More information about Papaji is available online at: http://www.realization.org/page/topics/poonja.htm, or: http://www.poonja.com.

These teachings came to my attention through the blessed Gangaji, a Western disciple of Papaji; and I also recommend her books, tapes, and satsangs. I will always be in her debt for this resource of Ramana's teachings she has given me. The love I feel for her because of this brings tears to my eyes and swiftness to my spirit-inspired fingers as I type this book. Thank you, Gangaji, for being such a wonderful bridge between the East and the West, thank you for bringing Ramana into my awareness. Gangaji's website is: www.gangaji.org.

Marshall Rosenberg and Nonviolent Communication

Marshall B. Rosenberg is the creator and developer of the most powerful communication model on Earth. This simple technique is extremely effective in problem solving and conflict resolution, especially in intimate relationships. Based on a realistic use of feelings as signals that identify the real needs and intention of any communication, this system is an honest approach at accepting oneself and others in spite of personal differences. Clear and eloquent, *Nonviolent Communication, A Language of Life* by Marshall B. Rosenberg, Ph.D., is a landmark book about how to talk.

This system is easy to learn and apply, and it gets results. It will open you up to a better communication not only with others but especially with your self. NVC has been the most effective communication tool I have ever come across, much better than "active listening" or "NLP" ("Neurolinguistic Programming"), NVC is a technique for real communication during all the hardest moments of any relationship. This model is essential for understanding how to communicate in important relationships and situations and will address all the problem areas of communication breakdowns. Nonviolent Communication workshops and centers and further information may be found online at: www.cnvc. org.

Kelly Bryson, MFT, a student of Marshal Rosenberg, has written a handbook for compassionate communication called, *Don't Be Nice, Be Real*, which I feel even more eloquently applies NVC techniques to the most typical relationship problems. Kelly addresses the issues and attitudes necessary to apply NVC with truthfulness and radical honesty. He shows with stories and metaphors exactly how compassionate communication works and why. I highly recommend his book as it gives a more personal and practical approach to non-violent communication. Kelly's website: www.languageofcompassion.com.

TEILHARD DE CHARDIN

Teilhard De Chardin was the most radical Jesuit visionary ever in the Catholic Church. His theories would have gotten him burned at the stake during the Inquisition; but raised in the era of emerging Darwinism, Teilhard expounded evolutionary concepts, which he claimed did not deny the real message of the Church. His mystical views of Christ stressed the importance in understanding that the "return of the Christ" involved all of humanity as Christ's head, and the Earth as his body.

Scorned by the Church for his scientific views, and by the scientists for his religious views, Teilhard is more popular posthumously than during his lifetime. As a scientist in anthropology, archaeology, botany, and biology; Teilhard explored the world; most famously as a participant in the "Peking Man" discovery and study; but it is his theories on evolution that bring him the most recognition today.

Antiquated and buried in used bookstores or online at Amazon and ebay, you will have to track down his books which were limited in publication and are mostly out of print.

Teilhard De Chardin's books include: *The Phenomenon of Man, Letters from a Traveller, The Divine Milieu, The Future of Man, Human Energy, Activation of Energy,* and *Hymn of the Universe.*

I feel *Activation of Energy* is the most revealing and least Catholic; it is a collection of his essays and letters starting in the late 1930s with his comments on the impending World War and going through the 1950s up to his death. In its almost archaic language, it describes his evolutionary and visionary philosophy clearly. The chapter on the war is amazing and it is appropriate still today.

These websites have excellent information on teilhard De Chardin:

www2.gol.com/users/coynerhm/teilhard.html

noosphere.cc/teilhardmenu.html

STEPHEN W. HAWKING

Stephen W. Hawking holds Newton's chair as Lucasian Professor of Mathematics at Cambridge University; and has authored: *A Brief History of Time, The Universe in a Nutshell,* and *The Theory of Everything.* These easy-to-understand explanations of science's state-of-the-art theories and discoveries have made the *New York Times'* bestseller list. Hawking has a thoroughly enjoyable style in his books and the information he shares is definitely mind-expanding, be ready for an altered state. His perspectives of the universe and humans is the result of researching almost all the scientific data available up to this point. His conclusions are inspirational and hopeful.

These books are Hawking's contribution to our human collective information pool, but they are also a clever way to bring the realms of theoretical science to the masses of humanity. Hawking manages to use words that lay people can understand. His descriptions of such complex things as how stars are formed, seem so simple and obvious, yet when considered, they bring a profound sense of the immense mystery of the universe.

I highly recommend all of Stephen W. Hawking's books as essential for really knowing the universe we came from and live in. He is one of the great geniuses of all time. Get his books at almost any bookstore or online. His website is: www.hawking.org.uk.

MILTON H. ERICKSON

The ultimate genius of the human mind's subconscious communication patterns was Milton H. Erickson. The story of his life is amazing; but, setting aside all he had to overcome to get there, Erickson became the originator of the American Clinical Hypnosis Institute. He is single handedly responsible for the American Medical Association eventually accepting hypnosis as a valid healing intervention rather than a vaudeville act. His results in therapy counselling were absolutely amazing, and so were his public lectures and demonstrations. Milton H. Erickson could hypnotise a whole room of people simultaneously or the most hardened sceptic in the blink of an eye. His command of language became legendary.

Bandler and Grinder modeled their famous Neurolinguistic Programming (NLP) system on his techniques. In the last years of his life, he limited his time to teaching professional psychologists and psychiatrists through therapy sessions he conducted on them. His influence is deep and profound in our understanding of how the unconscious and subconscious mind works. More importantly, he identified the trance language techniques to use in translating communication between the conscious and the unconscious. This has enabled an exponential use of hypnosis by practitioners who can now use these healing techniques successfully.

My favorite book by Milton H. Erickson is *My Voice Will Go With You*. It needs no understanding of professional psychiatry or psychology to read, and it reveals in his own down-home style how his words were so effective. Excellent for just flipping through and checking out the stories.

Books and information about Milton H. Erickson are online at:

www.erickson-foundation.org

www.miltonherickson.com

www.thechangeworks.com/index.html

R. BUCKMINSTER FULLER

Perhaps the most well known for his geodesic domes, R. Buckminster Fuller invented and patented more than can be listed here. As a design engineer and a social, technological, and systems analyst, Fuller wrote many books. The works of R. Buckminster Fuller became known to me in the 1960s. He and Marshall McLuhan were the only popular writers at the time describing our technological world from perspectives different from the old ways of seeing things. McLuhan focussed on media primarily, and was the first to get us thinking about how our technological mass media and communications systems were a message in themselves: "The medium is the message," he said. For more information see: http://www. marshallmcluhan.com.

R. Buckminster Fuller, however, had a broader scope and vision. He saw the trends, the evolution, and the history of humanity as reaching a point of *Utopia or Oblivion*, the title of one of his best books. But it is *Critical Path*, his last and most detailed critique, which is his masterpiece. In this book we are presented with his life's work, and his thoughts about the directions of our world. Fuller's analysis of history is enlightening and his metaphors describe the economic and political systems for what they are. Essential chapters in the book are: "Speculative Prehistory of Humanity," "Legally Piggily," "World Game," and "Critical Path: Part One, Two, Three, and Four."

The ideas presented and the histories related are important for anyone who wants to grasp the big picture of what it takes for humanity to live on Earth now and in the future. If you ever read anything of R. Buckminster Fuller's works this one, *Critical Path*, should be it; but it is very meaty stuff, so take your time and absorb the information; it really helps see the importance of change, especially with all that has happened in our world since its first printing in 1981.

Today more than ever, people should avail themselves of this wisdom from one of the greatest geniuses of all time. Still relevant and pertinent, Fuller's works continue to have a major impact; his inventions and ideas are based upon the needs of humanity to survive in harmony with the Earth and itself. His solutions are broadreaching and challenging, but in the end, his proofs are irrufutable: there is no other course for humanity's existence.

More information and books by or about R. Buckminster Fuller can be found at: www.bfi.org.

GARY ZUKAV

Gary Zukav, acclaimed author of *The Seat of the Soul*, has presented a fresh approach to the current stage of human evolution. A trained scientist and philosopher, Gary came up with new perspectives about many human dynamics that redefine where humanity is currently at and where it is evolving to. Perhaps the most important attitude shift he presents is the difference between "external power" and "authentic power." Gary describes in detail how this external power is the old paradigm; and how true, authentic power is the shift of awareness in humans that is now revealing more mature, harmonious ways of relating to our world.

Going beyond the five senses, authentic power tunes into the spiritual perceptions and recognises that true power is always inside us and not externally imposed. With well written and inspirational insights into the changes going on now, Gary describes how to access this authentic power within each of us.

His other books in the series, *The Heart of the Soul* and *The Mind of the Soul* continue with his observations on the human emotional and mental aspects being evolved by the spiritual energy presently manifesting world-wide. Full of techniques and exercises, these books explain and demonstrate how to catch and surf the tsunami wave of human consciousness now upon the Earth. The suggested exercises are powerful and revealing. Gary's first book, *Dancing Wu Li Masters*, gained him lots of attention for his mystical assesment of current science, but it is *The Seat of the Soul* which is the most powerful, advancing new attitudes about the body and soul of humanity. Gary's website is: www.zukav.com.

Dancing in the Shadow of Tyranny

Paramahansa Yogananda and the Self-Realization Fellowship

Paramahansa Yogananda was sent by his guru, Sri Yukteswar, to America, and the West, to spread the teachings of kriya yoga, the yoga of breath meditation. Yogananda was the first yogi to gain world-wide popularity, and his affect on the West has permanently established meditation centers around the planet. Kriya yoga is the most powerful meditation technique I have ever experienced. For over thirty-five years it has been my salvation in stopping my mind and centering my being.

The Autobiography of a Yogi, by Yogananda, is perhaps the yoga book which has sold more than any other. It was the first I ever read about the Indian systems. I suggest everyone read this book, it describes values and ways of life typical to a yogi, but more than that it is a history of one yogi's evolution. Yoganada also records in this book his meetings around the world with exceptional saints who exhibited miraculous powers. The descriptions are thrilling and revealing, they leave one with a deep respect and appreciation for the power of yoga and mystical commitment.

Yogananda also established the Self-Realisation Fellowship (SRF) in 1920, which has been teaching kriya yoga through many centers ever since. The SRF continues the work of Yogananda and publishes his books. It is one of the most powerful yoga groups in the world and has touched the lives of millions of people.

Sri Yukteswar wrote *The Holy Science*, which I recommend to intellectual folks as he was a raja yogi, one who studies the yoga of the mind. It is short but packed with concentrated nuggets that take many meditations to assimilate. But the power of vibration and the word "Om" is revealed in it so well and scientifically that you will constantly check out the 1892 date of the document in disbelief. Sri Yukteswar's understanding of atomic energy is astounding for his time. In the preface of the book, he talks about meeting the famous Himalayan saint, Babaji, who instructed him to set straight the yugas, According to this document and its explanation of vedic astrology, we are not in Kali yuga as the krishnas and other vedic scholars think. Sri Yukteswar explains the history of how the reckoning of the true astrological ages was lost and then reveals the true yuga now to be

Dwapara. For those who get hung up on the Kali-yuga reckoning, which is depressingly cynical about where humanity's evolution is at, this book will set you right.

The influence on my life from these teachers is priceless, I will always have a love and appreciation for them. Visit SRF centers, read Yogananda's books, try kriya yoga for meditation, and check out their website: www.yogananda-srf.org.

The Final Elimination of the Source of Fear by Saratoga and Telstar

This is the most powerful book you never heard of. Absolutely essential to understanding evolution, omnipresence, sex, and the current state of humanity. This book changed my life in one reading. The attitudes presented show a new way of looking at ourselves.

Fear is revealed completely, its source is studied in a manner that truly gets disempowered. The guided imagery, meditations, and metaphors lead one gently into the process of eliminating fear from our world and lives. The cosmic picture painted by Telstar and Saratoga shows how fear evolved and how it continues, but more importantly it describes the technique to deal with it.

Omnipresence is defined in a way that is experienced as you read about it. The tools given in this book are unique and more powerful than any self-help system. The information you will receive will help change the perceptions you have been stuck in. The book is powerful and should be read all the way through for the full benefit.

I highly recommend this book because it has an impact that the soul feels and responds to. *The Final Elimination of the Source of Fear* is a one-of-a-kind book and is not usually found in bookstores. Telstar and Saratoga offer more information on their website, including an actual ongoing event dealing with creating sexual stability which you can register for. I have not taken the event, but I have heard from participants that it is extremely powerful. The book alone is worth getting because of the deep impact it has. You can check out their website and purchase the book there: www.telstarnova.com.

DAN EVEHEMA AND THE HOPI

The Hopi Survival Kit by Dan Evehema and Thomas E. Mails clearly gives the real message of the traditional Hopi. This book is absolutely essential in understanding what the Hopi have to say that we should listen to. They believe the most important thing to work on now is the human attitude that thinks it knows better than others and imposes its will. I believe they are right.

The authors' second book, *Hotevilla, Hopi Shrine of the Covenant, Macrocosm of the World*, is the most complete record of the Hopi plight in existence. The history of the traditionals and the prophecy they carried are detailed. the communication of the elders through a newsletter as the white man's tribal government was imposed makes it clear that these indigenous people have the most solid claim to territory and sovereignty of them all.

The records of how the Hopi were the last holdouts to the white man's enculturation process are presented, along with the observations of the decline in the Hopi culture. The understanding you might receive from reading this will give you a bigger picture of how the US fuel industry has steamrolled the Native American culture and our environment.

I found personally that this was the most important Native American book ever published on their plight. Its archiving of the Hopi elders' teachings is priceless and the little-known history of Yukiuma and Hotevilla is the most relevant today of all the atrocities of the American enculturation processes imposed on Native Americans. The beauty and culture that once was Hotevilla is fading rapidly, but the historical record from the natives themselves is now available to all humanity. Check out what the prophecies have to say and why the Hopi finally came forward to reveal them. These books are available online or through your bookstore. Information about Dan Evehema online at: www.osfa.org.uk, www.wolflodge.org, and www.mytwobeadsworth.com.

DANCING IN THE SHADOW OF TYRANNY

THE EMPEROR WEARS NO CLOTHES BY JACK HERER

Subtitled, "Hemp and the Marijuana Conspiracy," this landmark book has been a best-seller for a few dozen years. Regularly updated with new research and new-found historical records, this compendium of facts and information about the world's number one natural resource has it all. It delineates the history of the illegal laws against marijuana and lists all the facts and proofs about it. Scientific, industrial, and medicinal research is included. Stories and anecdotes peppered among the articles and illustrations help relieve the strain of so much information.

This is *the* book and Jack Herer is *the* man who led the propaganda fight against the pot laws. Training thousands of petitioners and fighting numerous court battles, Jack Herer is the one person most responsible for the hemp revolution and the vast amount of information now available about hemp. I personally worked with Jack and videotaped him at work, he is a fireball of energy and commitment. He has challenged many activists to get real and inspired them to be bold. He has done his job well and his book is essential for understanding the reality of the war on hemp. Jack's website is: www.jackherer.com.

AWAKENING THE SLEEPING BUDDHA BY THE TWELFTH TAI SITUPA

This book is the best on Buddha's teachings that I ever read. The descriptions of the essentials and the details of the techniques are elucidated with the true heart of Buddha himself. The poetic, yet philosophically revealing, insights of the Twelfth Tai Situpa are so real that they resonate with the Buddha inside us easily and naturally. The Tai Situpa's love for Buddha's teachings is obvious, yet in an unromanticized manner, he explains so clearly that the lessons begin to cause an exponential understanding of the Buddha's teachings within the mind and heart of the reader. This book is the secret hidden gem of all Buddhist books, for it reveals Buddha to the reader in a way that they can feel his presence.

If you are interested in really knowing what Buddha meant by his words, you are in for a treat with this book, it will seem like the Buddha within you speaking in a personal way that you can understand. Available in stores or directly from Shambala Publications at: www.shambala.com.

THE LAZY MAN'S GUIDE TO ENLIGHTENMENT BY THADDEUS GOLAS

This thin book is the ultimate for lazy folks, especially of the hippie persuasion. Originally written in 1972, this classic is still available; search online bookstores for it. Short yet brilliantly written, this book reveals the path without all the mumbo-jumbo. Simple, common-sense, practical, and empowering, *The Lazy Man's Guide to Enlightenment* is the easiest mystical manual to read. I was thrilled to find it in the 1970s and I still read it. Thoroughly enjoyable even with its slightly "flower-child" wording.

MAHATMA GANDHI

The most famous of the non-violent activists and the leader of the non-violent resistence to English rule over India is Mahatma Gandhi. This man has influenced most of the activists I ever met. His philosophy of "Ahimsa" is important to the evolution of humanity. Any and all of his books are worthy of reading. Please take the time to get familiar with this great saint's mind. At www.mkgandhi.org, www.gandhiinstitute.org, or web.mahatma.org.in.

RAMAKRISHNA

Ramakrishna was so devoted to God and the Goddess that just reading *Great Swan* by Lex Hixon will bring shivers of devotional ecstacy to most sincere lovers of the divine. The aspect of devotion is an important part of the mystical path, it allows the heart to achieve bliss and conscious union with divinity. I personally use bhakti, mantra, and kirtan because I enjoy the experience of divine presence; and these practices bring the awareness of the divinity always present into the body, heart, and mind. Ramakrishna was constantly swimming in the bliss of devotional awareness, and his life and words are a delight to experience. More information at: www.ramakrishna.org.

"WHAT THE BLEEP DO WE KNOW?"

This movie is absolutely essential if you want to see the real tip of the human-consciousness-science iceberg. An independant film that is now playing at small theaters because of the huge interest spread by word of mouth about it, it is absolutely amazing! Check out where it is playing from their website: www.whatthebleep.com.

REBUILDING AMERICA'S DEFENSES: STRATEGY, FORCES AND RESOURCES FOR A NEW CENTURY

If you do not believe the military-industrial complex is blatantly attempting world domination and control, you must read this document they wrote. It is available on Ray Taliaferro's webite. Ray is the best left-wing radical government watchdog of the talk show hosts, on for over 25 years late night, KGO AM 810. You can download the PDF at: www.raytal.com.

FACING LOVE ADDICTION BY PIA MELLODY

This is the main book on codependency that I would recommend; it has the clearest presentation and covers the very heart of all codependency techniques. This book reveals the secret that most codependency is based on the model formed by the "love addict" and the "avoidance addict." We all fall in and out of codependent behaviors everyday to various degrees. But those who stay stuck in the patterns are usually love or avoidance addicts *and they tend to pair with the other: Love addicts get involved with avoidance addicts.* People may be both addicted to love and avoidance, and so behave in extremely confusing schizophrenic ways.

I highly recommend this book; it nails these behaviors on the head. Once you understand how the push-me pull-you dynamics work between love and avoidance addicts, you will see how and why the pattern gets continually repeated. These two addiction states are the basis for almost all codependent forms of behavior. To deal with these sorts of stuck places of codependent compulsive-obsessive behaviors takes first recognizing we *are* codependent and then taking responsibility for our experience. Without these two steps nothing will ever change the pattern.

It was this book that helped me recognize my love addiction and begin to change. I believe this is the one book anyone who wonders whether they are in a codependent relationship should read. Really, even if you don't think you are codependent you should read this just so you will recognize the pitfalls and tendencies of falling into codependent behavior—no matter to what degree.

Love addiction is as dangerous and unhealthy as avoidance addiction, but the two together in a relationship is the most toxic of all codependent forms because they keep feeding the other more fuel to stay stuck and dysfunctional. Mellody's website is www.piamellody.com.

THE ASSISI DECALOGUE FOR PEACE

1. We commit ourselves to proclaiming our firm conviction that violence and terrorism are incompatible with the authentic spirit of religion, and, as we condemn every recourse to violence and war in the name of God or of religion, we commit ourselves to doing everything possible to eliminate the root causes of terrorism.

2. We commit ourselves to educating people to mutual respect and esteem, in order to help bring about a peaceful and fraternal coexistence between people of different ethnic groups, cultures and religions.

3. We commit ourselves to fostering the culture of dialogue, so that there will be an increase of understanding and mutual trust between individuals and among peoples, for these are the premise of authentic peace.

4. We commit ourselves to defending the right of everyone to live a decent life in accordance with their own cultural identity, and to form freely a family of his own.

5. We commit ourselves to frank and patient dialogue, refusing to consider our differences as an insurmountable barrier, but recognizing

instead that to encounter the diversity of others can become an opportunity for greater reciprocal understanding.

6. We commit ourselves to forgiving one another for past and present errors and prejudices, and to supporting one another in a common effort both to overcome selfishness and arrogance, hatred and violence, and to learn from the past that peace without justice is no true peace.

7. We commit ourselves to taking the side of the poor and the helpless, to speaking out for those who have no voice and to working effectively to change these situations, out of the conviction that no one can be happy alone.

8. We commit ourselves to taking up the cry of those who refuse to be resigned to violence and evil, and we are desire to make every effort possible to offer the men and women of our time real hope for justice and peace.

9. We commit ourselves to encouraging all efforts to promote friendship between peoples, for we are convinced that, in the absence of solidarity and understanding between peoples, technological progress exposes the world to a growing risk of destruction and death.

10. We commit ourselves to urging leaders of nations to make every effort to create and consolidate, on the national and international levels, a world of solidarity and peace based on justice.

The Vatican's link for information on the Assisi Decalogue: www.vatican.va/holy_father/john_paul_ii/letters/2002/documents/hf_jp-ii_let_20020304_capi-stato_en.html

THE BILL OF RIGHTS OF THE US CONSITUTION

This document is absolutely essential in understandiing the intentions of our country in forming its original government. The loss of these freedoms is a loss of our rights. To know them and use them is really the "American way."

Amendment I

Congress shall make no law respecting an establishment of religion, or prohibiting the free exercise thereof; or abridging the freedom of speech, or of the press; or the right of the people peaceably to assemble, and to petition the government for a redress of grievances.

Amendment II

A well regulated militia, being necessary to the security of a free state, the right of the people to keep and bear arms, shall not be infringed.

Amendment III

No soldier shall, in time of peace be quartered in any house, without the consent of the owner, nor in time of war, but in a manner to be prescribed by law.

Amendment IV

The right of the people to be secure in their persons, houses, papers, and effects, against unreasonable searches and seizures, shall not be violated, and no warrants shall issue, but upon probable cause, supported by oath or affirmation, and particularly describing the place to be searched, and the persons or things to be seized.

Amendment V

No person shall be held to answer for a capital, or otherwise infamous crime, unless on a presentment or indictment of a grand jury, except in cases arising in the land or naval forces, or in the militia, when in actual service in time of war or public danger; nor shall any person be subject for the same offense to be twice put in jeopardy of life or limb; nor shall be compelled in any criminal case to be a witness against himself, nor be deprived of life, liberty, or property, without due process of law; nor shall private property be taken for public use, without just compensation.

Amendment VI

In all criminal prosecutions, the accused shall enjoy the right to a speedy and public trial, by an impartial jury of the state and district wherein the crime shall have been committed, which district shall have been previously ascertained by law, and to be informed of the nature and cause of the accusation; to be confronted with the witnesses against him; to have compulsory process for obtaining witnesses in his favor, and to have the assistance of counsel for his defense.

Amendment VII

In suits at common law, where the value in controversy shall exceed twenty dollars, the right of trial by jury shall be preserved, and no fact tried by a jury, shall be otherwise reexamined in any court of the United States, than according to the rules of the common law.

Amendment VIII

Excessive bail shall not be required, nor excessive fines imposed, nor cruel and unusual punishments inflicted.

Amendment IX

The enumeration in the Constitution, of certain rights, shall not be construed to deny or disparage others retained by the people.

Amendment X

The powers not delegated to the United States by the Constitution, nor prohibited by it to the states, are reserved to the states respectively, or to the people.

Compare the United States' Bill of Rights with the following and see the evolutionary grasp of humanity for a declaration of rights which are supreme above any government or military force.

Universal Declaration of Human Rights
UN General Assembly, 1948

PREAMBLE

Whereas recognition of the inherent dignity and of the equal and inalienable rights of all members of the human family is the foundation of freedom, justice and peace in the world,

Whereas disregard and contempt for human rights have resulted in barbarous acts which have outraged the conscience of mankind, and the advent of a world in which human beings shall enjoy freedom of speech and belief and freedom from fear and want has been proclaimed as the highest aspiration of the common people,

Whereas it is essential, if man is not to be compelled to have recourse, as a last resort, to rebellion against tyranny and oppression, that human rights should be protected by the rule of law,

Whereas it is essential to promote the development of friendly relations between nations,

Whereas the peoples of the United Nations have in the Charter reaffirmed their faith in fundamental human rights, in the dignity and worth of the human person and in the equal rights of men and women and have determined to promote social progress and better standards of life in larger freedom,

Whereas Member States have pledged themselves to achieve, in cooperation with the United Nations, the promotion of universal respect for and observance of human rights and fundamental freedoms,

Whereas a common understanding of these rights and freedoms is of the greatest importance for the full realization of this pledge,

Now, therefore,

The General Assembly,

Proclaims this Universal Declaration of Human Rights as a common standard of achievement for all peoples and all nations, to the end that every individual and every organ of society, keeping this Declaration constantly in mind, shall strive by teaching and education to promote respect for these rights and freedoms and by progressive measures, national and international, to secure their universal and effective recognition and observance, both among the peoples of Member States themselves and among the peoples of territories under their jurisdiction.

Article 1

All human beings are born free and equal in dignity and rights. They are endowed with reason and conscience and should act towards one another in a spirit of brotherhood.

Article 2

Everyone is entitled to all the rights and freedoms set forth in this Declaration, without distinction of any kind, such as race, colour, sex, language, religion, political or other opinion, national or social origin, property, birth or other status.

Furthermore, no distinction shall be made on the basis of the political, jurisdictional or international status of the country or territory to which a person belongs, whether it be independent, trust, non-self-governing or under any other limitation of sovereignty.

Article 3

Everyone has the right to life, liberty and security of person.

Article 4

No one shall be held in slavery or servitude; slavery and the slave trade shall be prohibited in all their forms.

Article 5

No one shall be subjected to torture or to cruel, inhuman or degrading treatment or punishment.

Article 6

Everyone has the right to recognition everywhere as a person before the law.

Article 7

All are equal before the law and are entitled without any discrimination to equal protection of the law. All are entitled to equal protection against any discrimination in violation of this Declaration and against any incitement to such discrimination.

Article 8

Everyone has the right to an effective remedy by the competent national tribunals for acts violating the fundamental rights granted him by the constitution or by law.

Article 9

No one shall be subjected to arbitrary arrest, detention or exile.

Article 10

Everyone is entitled in full equality to a fair and public hearing by an independent and impartial tribunal, in the determination of his rights and obligations and of any criminal charge against him.

Article 11

1. Everyone charged with a penal offence has the right to be presumed innocent until proved guilty according to law in a public trial at which he has had all the guarantees necessary for his defence.

2. No one shall be held guilty of any penal offence on account of any act or omission which did not constitute a penal offence, under national or international law, at the time when it was committed. Nor shall a heavier penalty be imposed than the one that was applicable at the time the penal offence was committed.

Article 12

No one shall be subjected to arbitrary interference with his privacy, family, home or correspondence, nor to attacks upon his honour and reputation. Everyone has the right to the protection of the law against such interference or attacks.

Article 13

1. Everyone has the right to freedom of movement and residence within the borders of each State.

2. Everyone has the right to leave any country, including his own, and to return to his country.

Article 14

1. Everyone has the right to seek and to enjoy in other countries asylum from persecution.

2. This right may not be invoked in the case of prosecutions genuinely arising from non-political crimes or from acts contrary to the purposes and principles of the United Nations.

Article 15

1. Everyone has the right to a nationality.

2. No one shall be arbitrarily deprived of his nationality nor denied the right to change his nationality.

Article 16

1. Men and women of full age, without any limitation due to race, nationality or religion, have the right to marry and to found a family. They are entitled to equal rights as to marriage, during marriage and at its dissolution.

2. Marriage shall be entered into only with the free and full consent of the intending spouses.

3. The family is the natural and fundamental group unit of society and is entitled to protection by society and the State.

Article 17

1. Everyone has the right to own property alone as well as in association with others.

2. No one shall be arbitrarily deprived of his property.

Article 18

Everyone has the right to freedom of thought, conscience and religion; this right includes freedom to change his religion or belief, and freedom, either alone or in community with others and in public or private, to manifest his religion or belief in teaching, practice, worship and observance.

Article 19

Everyone has the right to freedom of opinion and expression; this right includes freedom to hold opinions without interference and to seek, receive and impart information and ideas through any media and regardless of frontiers.

Article 20

1. Everyone has the right to freedom of peaceful assembly and association.

2. No one may be compelled to belong to an association.

Article 21

1. Everyone has the right to take part in the government of his country, directly or through freely chosen representatives.

2. Everyone has the right to equal access to public service in his country.

3. The will of the people shall be the basis of the authority of government; this will shall be expressed in periodic and genuine elections which

shall be by universal and equal suffrage and shall be held by secret vote or by equivalent free voting procedures.

Article 22

Everyone, as a member of society, has the right to social security and is entitled to realization, through national effort and international co-operation and in accordance with the organization and resources of each State, of the economic, social and cultural rights indispensable for his dignity and the free development of his personality.

Article 23

1. Everyone has the right to work, to free choice of employment, to just and favourable conditions of work and to protection against unem-ployment.

2. Everyone, without any discrimination, has the right to equal pay for equal work.

3. Everyone who works has the right to just and favourable remunera-tion ensuring for himself and his family an existence worthy of human dignity, and supplemented, if necessary, by other means of social protec-tion.

4. Everyone has the right to form and to join trade unions for the protection of his interests.

Article 24

Everyone has the right to rest and leisure, including reasonable limita-tion of working hours and periodic holidays with pay.

Article 25

1. Everyone has the right to a standard of living adequate for the health and well-being of himself and of his family, including food, cloth-ing, housing and medical care and necessary social services, and the right to security in the event of unemployment, sickness, disability, widowhood, old age or other lack of livelihood in circumstances beyond his control.

2. Motherhood and childhood are entitled to special care and assis-tance. All children, whether born in or out of wedlock, shall enjoy the same social protection.

Article 26

1. Everyone has the right to education. Education shall be free, at least in the elementary and fundamental stages. Elementary education shall be compulsory. Technical and professional education shall be made generally available and higher education shall be equally accessible to all on the basis of merit.

2. Education shall be directed to the full development of the human personality and to the strengthening of respect for human rights and

fundamental freedoms. It shall promote understanding, tolerance and friendship among all nations, racial or religioUS groups, and shall further the activities of the United Nations for the maintenance of peace.

3. Parents have a prior right to choose the kind of education that shall be given to their children.

Article 27

1. Everyone has the right freely to participate in the cultural life of the community, to enjoy the arts and to share in scientific advancement and its benefits.

2. Everyone has the right to the protection of the moral and material interests resulting from any scientific, literary or artistic production of which he is the author.

Article 28

Everyone is entitled to a social and international order in which the rights and freedoms set forth in this Declaration can be fully realized.

Article 29

1. Everyone has duties to the community in which alone the free and full development of his personality is possible.

2. In the exercise of his rights and freedoms, everyone shall be subject only to such limitations as are determined by law solely for the purpose of securing due recognition and respect for the rights and freedoms of others and of meeting the just requirements of morality, public order and the general welfare in a democratic society.

3. These rights and freedoms may in no case be exercised contrary to the purposes and principles of the United Nations.

Article 30

Nothing in this Declaration may be interpreted as implying for any State, group or person any right to engage in any activity or to perform any act aimed at the destruction of any of the rights and freedoms set forth herein.